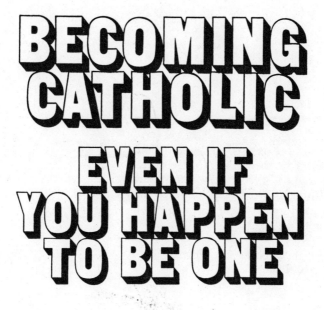

BECOMING CATHOLIC
EVEN IF YOU HAPPEN TO BE ONE

James J. Killgallon
Mary Michael O'Shaughnessy, O.P.
Gerard P. Weber

ACTA Foundation, Chicago, Illinois

Library of Congress Catalogue No. 79–89875

Printed in the United States   ISBN No. 0–914070–13–4

CONTENTS

PREFACE

Not so very long ago, if your name was Slominski, O'Brien, or Antonucci, either you were a Roman Catholic or there was "something wrong." Being a Catholic, for most people, was a matter of having been baptized into the Church as an infant because they had been born of Catholic parents. Those who, as adults, had freely chosen to become Catholics were called *converts,* and the word was used only for such people.

Today, the situation is changing. In many cases it has already changed. Most Catholics still do insist that their children be baptized as infants and make every effort to raise their children as Catholics. More and more, however, those children, as they grow older, feel quite free to question whether they really want to be held to that early commitment made for them by others. Lifelong adult Catholics, too, are reexamining and reappraising their commitment to the Church.

The result of all this is sometimes a quiet withdrawal into the ranks of what has been rather aptly called "retired Catholics." Such a withdrawal can be an outright break with the Church—accompanied either by resentment and anger or with bittersweet nostalgia. More often (and this is an encouraging sign) such reexamination and reappraisal can lead to a new, more adult, and more responsible attitude towards the faith and the Catholic Church.

More and more Catholics are becoming aware that being Catholic is not a matter of mere intellectual acceptance of a set of dogmas or compliance with certain practices. They are beginning to realize that Catholicism is a way of life which, while demanding, is richly fulfilling and rewarding— one which gives new meaning and new zest to their lives.

The words we use today in connection with the Faith have come in for some reexamination and some reappraisal, too. Words such as *convert* and *instructions in the Faith* have a meaning today that is richer and more extensive. Conversion is seen not as a once-in-a-lifetime event which happens only to adults who join the Church. Rather, it is seen as a process which is lifelong and which takes place again and again on ever deepening levels. Becoming Catholic is seen as a gradual process by which one enters more and more deeply into the thought, life, prayer, and mission of that body which is the most ancient, most widespread, and (to the surprise of many) most varied of the Christian communions.

Instructions in the Faith are seen not merely as periods of indoctrination in which the objective truth of the various articles of faith is demonstrated. Rather, instructions include an acceptance of these truths into one's life. It is no longer just a question of showing that this sacrament or that doctrine is valid and true but of helping the catechumen or lifelong Catholic see what meaning this sacrament or that doctrine has for his or her life.

Becoming Catholic is a book for those who want to deepen their understanding of and make more meaningful their membership in the Catholic Church. It is offered to those who are "looking into" the Church, to lifelong Catholics who want to go deeper, to "retired Catholics," and to those who may have become inactive or opted out and now may be willing to take another, more adult look at the Church. **Becoming Catholic** is a book, not a catechism. A catechism, traditionally, covers *everything*. This book deals with basic, essential doctrines. Moreover, despite its concentration on content, this book emphasizes *attitude* towards Catholic belief, rather than authoritative statements and memorization. Those who desire a complete catechetical treatment can refer to the many catechisms which are available.

Becoming Catholic is designed for use by either individuals or groups—usually with someone to act as a director or guide. We avoid the word *instructor* or *priest* for two reasons. First, the one who performs this function today is, often enough, a deacon, a lay minister, or a religious. Secondly, we wish to get away from the notion that the whole process is simply a matter of imparting information or of explaining doctrine in a wholly objective way. For these reasons, we use the word director for this person.

How to Use the Book

Each Chapter of **Becoming Catholic** is made up of five sections: The Essay, Questions, Responses, The Christian Community, and the Personal Profile. Each of these elements is presented in slightly different ways throughout the book.

   1.   The Essay. The dogmatic material that is the subject of the chapter is presented in the *Essay* which opens each chapter. There are a number of ways to work with the *Essay* in each chapter.

- The people can read the *Essay* beforehand and after sharing their answers to any questions that may have arisen, they can discuss the material in the *Essay* with the director. The director can go over the material to amplify and clarify it.
- The people need not read the material beforehand. Instead, the director reads the *Essay,* explains it, and comments on it.

In either case, a subsequent reading of the *Essay* will be helpful.

2. The Questions. The *Questions* bring the matter explained in the *Essay* into the lives and experiences of the people. These *Questions* are not like the old catechism questions which were devices to highlight a doctrinal point, give a succinct answer, and be simple to memorize. The *Questions* in this book are devices to relate the content to one's experiences and to help people incorporate the ideas into their daily lives. The *Questions,* therefore, follow a pattern throughout the book: "What problems might be expected? How can one deal with these problems?"

In order to avoid giving the impression that these are devices which give a definitive, dogmatic answer, the *Responses* to the *Questions* are separated from the individual *Questions* in the text.

The *Questions* given in the text are meant to stimulate and give direction to a discussion. Different persons and different groups will find certain questions more pertinent. So, groups and individuals can use the *Questions* as they see fit. An important feature of this part of each chapter is the peoples' own response—how they feel or have felt on this point, what fears or apprehensions they may have, what suggestions they have as to the handling of their fears, etc. Therefore, there should be latitude in discussing this part of the chapter. The important thing is that the people become thoroughly involved in this part and that the discussion be related both to the matter under consideration and to the thoughts, feelings, experiences, and expectations of each person. Here it is particularly important that the director facilitate rather than instruct.

3. The Responses. The *Responses* are brief passages which explicate and delineate the answers to the *Questions*. The *Questions* should always be asked in groups as they are presented in the book, and the participants should always give their answers *before* reading or discussing the *Responses*. Very often the participants will touch on the points mentioned in the *Responses*. As a result, it will not be necessary to go into the *Responses* in any great detail. At times, participants will mention points not in the *Responses* and thereby enrich the group. In no case should the *Questions* be asked and the *Responses* read or explained before the people have had a chance to talk.

After the discussion of each set of *Questions*, the director may wish to expand on the answers of the participants by speaking with them about the material in the *Responses*. Or the director may merely indicate points in the *Responses* that were not reflected in the people's answers. In either case, the director should encourage as much dialog as possible about the *Questions* and the *Responses*.

4. The Christian Community. Because the Catholic Faith is meaningless unless it is grounded in the believing community—the Church, each chapter contains a special section which relates the material in the *Essay*, the *Questions*, and the *Responses* to the experiences, customs, rituals, and life of the Church.

5. The Personal Profile. In order that the whole experience of **Becoming Catholic** might become a conscious source of growth for the participants, the *Personal Profile* is an integral part of each chapter. The *Personal Profile* is an opportunity for the people using this book to record their feelings and experiences in the chapter, to use the material in the chapter as a source of prayer, and to look ahead to what is still to come by recording their reactions to various questions and situations. To this end, the *Personal Profile* is divided into three parts.

- **The Review.** The *Review* is a series of questions to help the participants be sure that they have understood and reacted to the basic material of the chapter. Not all the points covered in the chapter are in the *Review*, but the main idea is there. It would seem best that the participants do the *Review* before they leave the session so that they may record their immediate reactions and ask questions of the director if they have missed the main idea of the chapter.

- **Prayer.** At the end of each chapter, there is a section containing references to Scripture which the people may use at the session, but more especially between sessions. These passages are meant to be a basis for prayer. They are a part of the *Profile* because prayer itself is a most important response to the material of each chapter. The director may select one or the other passage and use it as the basis for shared prayer at the end of each session.

- **The Preview.** At the very end of the *Profile* (and the chapter) there is a *Preview* of the material to be covered in the following chapter. The *Preview* should be a source of reflection and a preparation for a discussion of the next chapter. There are no correct or incorrect answers to the questions posed in the *Preview.* They are meant to elicit ideas and experiences. The important thing about the answers to these questions is how accurately they reflect how the participants think and what they have experienced. A director should simply raise the questions and encourage the people to express their feelings, experiences, and ideas about the topics freely and frankly. (NOTE: The *Preview* should be the first order of business in each session.)

Time

A time limit for the session should be agreed upon at the outset. Free and open discussion is of the essence. The sessions should be at least an hour long. An hour and a half would be even better, if practical. Enough time is needed to do justice to each of the sessions. Above and beyond that, however, there must be an agreement about time, and the agreement should be enforced. Otherwise a session could easily get out of hand.

The important thing is that the group goes over all the material. It is not necessary that the director go over each single point, as long as the participants do so in some way or other. The director may sometimes feel that discussion on one point or another becomes so good and fruitful that the material of a given session cannot be covered in the time agreed upon. In that event, the material of the session could be extended over two or even several sessions.

Private Reading

Becoming Catholic is meant to be read and discussed with a group or at least one other person. If you read it by yourself, try to follow the procedure of answering the *Preview,* the *Questions,* and the *Review.* Spend some time praying about the material presented.

Bible

It will be necessary to have and to use a Bible in conjunction with the text. Any good version will be satisfactory.

A BEGINNING

Welcome to High Adventure

A person who decides to investigate the Catholic faith is responding to a call to adventure. Whether the person is looking into Catholicism for the first time or, after many years of being a Catholic, is looking more deeply into what it means to be a Catholic, that person is responding to a call to embark on an adventure, to leave the security of known positions and to look into new ones, to take the risk of having his or her life changed in some way.

The early Christians spoke of those who embarked on this adventure as ones who looked into and embraced "The Way." When St. Paul obtained warrants to arrest Christians, he went about looking for "anyone he might find, man or woman, living according to *the new way" (Acts 9:2)*. Later, when he was preaching in Philippi, Paul met a clairvoyant girl who followed him shouting to all, "These men are the servants of the Most High God: they will make known to you a *way* of salvation" *(Acts 16:17)*. In Antioch, a Jew named Apollos who had been "instructed in the *new way* of the Lord," preached well but not fully. Priscilla and Aquila took him to their home and "explained to him God's *new way* in greater detail" *(Acts 18:24–28)*.

God calls all people to this great adventure—this journey or pilgrimage. He calls all to leave the safe and familiar and to launch into the deep, to take a risk, to change their way of life. We need knowledge—knowledge not only of the workings of God and of the teachings of the Church, but knowledge about ourselves as well.

True knowledge begins at home. The ancient Greek philosopher, Socrates, made this discovery and used it as the basis of his whole teaching. "Know thyself" was his starting point, and it was his firm conviction that unless one did come to know and understand oneself, one could never have a really good understanding of anything else. St. Augustine made the same discovery and carried it beyond philosophy into theology and the spiritual life. One cannot come to any real appreciation of God and one's relation to him, Augustine maintained, without self-knowledge. His constant prayer was, "Lord let me know myself, that I may know thee."

Those who are concerned with both human development and spiritual growth today are in complete agreement with these two wise men of antiquity. If anything, they are even more convinced that self-knowledge is at the very root of human development and spiritual growth.

This book is a book directed toward gaining the self-knowledge which is the necessary basis of conversion.

If we are to know anyone really well, we need to know something about the way that person thinks and feels. We also need to know something about the experiences he or she has had, because these have a bearing on the person's life and personality.

If we are interested in coming to know ourselves really well, we need to become very much aware of our *real* ideas, our *real* feelings, and we need to reflect on our experiences, especially those which have had a significant impact on our lives.

Therefore, involved as we are here with the process of conversion, we shall take these three items into consideration at every step. We shall be examining our ideas, comparing them with and measuring them against the teachings of Jesus Christ. We shall attend to and analyze our feelings

2

about ourselves, others, and God in order to gain an insight into our actual attitudes. And we shall recall and work from our experience, particularly the experience of God in our lives.

In the matter of self-knowledge, one of the key words is *actual*. What we assume we believe or say we believe is not always the same as our belief or basic assumptions about ourselves, our world, and God on which we act. There might well be a difference between the *real* goals which guide our way of acting, and the *stated* goals which we profess and express. The basic assumptions, the *real,* are often enough, not very clear and definite. They may be very well hidden in the background.

The challenge that faces us, then, is the challenge of growth—that is, the slow, step by step, but always interesting and even sometimes exciting process of getting our belief, our feelings, and our experiences together. This is a process of comparing the way we *think* about things with the way we *feel* about them, always in the light of and against the background of the experiences which have had an impact on us.

In each section of this book, therefore, we shall be dealing with all three—thoughts, feelings, and impact experiences. All three will be "on stage" at all times. But in different units or sessions, one of the three may take the center of the stage.

Over all, though, we shall be involved with bringing all three together. This means, in a positive and healing sense, that we will be involved with "getting *ourselves* more together."

And that is a high adventure!

1 Come Follow Me

It was early in the morning. Few of the followers of John the Baptist were up and about as yet. But the two fishermen were there, red-eyed and sleepy after a full night of fishing. Their names were John and Andrew. They would just spend a few minutes with this prophet, John, they thought, before making their way home and to bed.

But it didn't work out that way. Not today. This morning someone new had appeared on the scene. It was a man called Jesus. He smiled, waved a greeting to John and walked slowly on, along the bank of the River Jordan.

John caught the eyes of the two fishermen. He pointed to Jesus and said, "Behold the Lamb of God!"

Strange words. Intriguing words. The fishermen had heard of this Jesus—scattered reports, rumors that hinted that he might turn out to be a prophet. But these words of John the Baptist were something else—the "Lamb of God." By mutual, unspoken agreement, Andrew and John decided on the spot that they had to know more. They began to tag along after Jesus, half hoping, half fearing that they might come face to face with him, speak to him, ask him questions, learn something more about him.

Suddenly Jesus stopped. He turned around slowly. He had heard them, or sensed their presence. He knew they were following him. Now Andrew and John felt rather foolish. But Jesus was not annoyed. His eyes were smiling, even though his question was direct—"What do you want?" Those were the words, but the meaning, judging by the expression and tone of voice, was really, "What can I do for you?"

Andrew's mouth moved, but nothing came out. John blurted out the first thing that came to his mind. "Where do you live?" Again, those were the words, but the meaning, not yet expressed but deep within the minds of Andrew and John, was really—"We'd like to get to know you better."

Jesus' response was an open invitation, an invitation that would grow and expand day by day and year by year for a lifetime. But right now it was a simple, general invitation—"Come and see."

Andrew and John went with Jesus. They spent the whole day with him. And what they saw that day impressed them so much that each sought out his brother that evening and brought him to Jesus *(John 1:35–42)*.

On the face of it, it was curiosity that drew Andrew and John, that coupled with a natural response to what must have been the charm of Jesus' personality. But ultimately and underneath all this, it was the call, the call which the Father was giving through Jesus. Jesus was inviting them to open themselves up to God to become aware of the grace that comes from God and invites us to closer union with him and to growth in humanity and sanctity.

There must have been, in each man, a desire, a need, perhaps only dimly felt, for some deeper meaning to their lives, a desire for some further understanding of what they had always known and believed about God and their people. There may have been some dissatisfaction with the dull routine of their lives and a wish to see whether there wasn't something more that they could experience or become.

As Andrew and John responded to the invitation God gave through Jesus that morning, they did not really understand the invitation and its implications in their lives. Most probably they saw in Jesus no more than a pleasant, exciting, challenging personality, one that they would like to be associated with. By the end of the day they had come to think that here, possibly, was a great prophet, maybe even the political leader that many had come to hope for. But at this point they surely had no way of knowing that this Jesus they had just met was the Son of God. Nor could they know then that through Jesus they would come to greater intimacy with God, that they would come to understand God and themselves better and that their lives would be transformed.

Nor did this first encounter with Jesus mark a complete break with their former life. Andrew and John and the others who would eventually constitute the band of apostles continued to ply the trade of fishermen. Only as time went on and they became more closely associated with Jesus and more deeply involved with him, with one another, and with the work of Jesus among the people did they give up their occupations and their families and become full-time disciples of Jesus. Even during the years of Christ's public life and up to the time of Pentecost they did not see the full implications of Christ's personality or his mission and their part in that mission. *(Mark 8:14–21, John 2:22, John 16:12).*

In fact, even after Pentecost, their understanding of themselves and their mission was to grow only slowly and sometimes painfully day by day *(Acts 1:1–7, and chapters 6 to 15 throughout).*

Questions
- **How do we *experience* the call of God in our life?**
- ***To what* is God calling us in the call to conversion?**
- **How do we *respond* to God's call to conversion?**

The Experience

People experience the call of God in different ways, and a given person experiences it in different ways at different times. Each person receives invitations to grow in living according to the Gospel that are in line with that person's temperament, capabilities, general endowments, and background. Sometimes a thought comes from a passage in Scripture or in another book. Often an invitation is cloaked in a circumstance of life—a change of jobs, a family incident, or an occurrence which seems trivial or unconnected with spiritual growth but which may cause one to pause and consider or reflect upon later. It is almost invariably true that the call comes in relation to other people. God speaks to us through other persons, their words, actions, example, etc. Andrew and John met Jesus through John the Baptist. Their brothers came into contact with him through Andrew and John. Many of the people who came out to hear Jesus had heard about him from others. People of the next generation and those in other lands came in contact with Jesus through others who believed in him. Today, the call comes in much the same way. Both the call to learn about Jesus and his message and the call to become more deeply involved with him comes through others and through events in ordinary life.

These events are so ordinary, in fact, that rarely do we see in them the call of God, even though it is there. Actually, God is continually giving us his call in the events of our lives. Usually it is only later when something reminds us of an incident that we recall it and see a meaning we failed to see at the time. Then, we realize that the event was actually a call from God. It is at such times that we have an "ah ha!" experience—the moment of recognition, when we say to ourselves, "Of course! That's the way it was! That's what it meant!"

A Call—To What?

Ultimately, the call of God to conversion is a call to become a more complete and whole human being in relation to ourselves, to others, and to God. Specifically, to discern the direction in which God is summoning us we need to see where we are now, where we were, and what we find we are now doing. For example, we might be the kind of person who has been prone to be mistrustful of others and more fearful than loving in our attitude towards God. Then something happens which inclines us to overcome our fear and mistrust, to reach out to others and to God. When this sort of thing happens, we can come to realize that the event or experience which occasioned the changing attitude was a call of God summoning us from our attitude of mistrust and fear to one of more trust and love.

In general, we may say that the direction of God's call is from something which inhibits growth to something which frees us and promotes our growth:

- From fear to trust.
- From a magical notion of prayer marked by bargaining with God to obtain something to adult conversation with him.
- From being directed by others to taking responsibility for our own lives, acting on our own convictions, and trusting our own insights.
- From manipulating others to respecting the freedom of others.
- From self-centeredness and a "going it alone" attitude to willingness to work with others and concern for their welfare.
- From an attitude of looking down on others to one of respect and reverence for others.
- From an attitude of self deprecation to seeing ourselves as valuable and worthwhile.

The Response

We respond to God's calls or react to them in various ways. Sometimes we simply fail to recognize a call. Sometimes we become dimly or even sharply aware of a call and actually resist it, oppose it, act against it.

God's call is always an invitation. He leaves us free to accept, ignore, or reject it. Jesus gave an excellent example in his parable of the Sower and the Seed. The seed was scattered freely and generously and offered to the ground with liberality. What happened to it depended on how the various kinds of soil on which it fell received it (*Matthew 13:4–9*).

Those who respond positively do so in various ways and in varying degrees. But there is something that is common in every positive response to such a call.

There is an underlying desire to be a better person, to find a deeper meaning, to be happier, more at peace. People who respond positively to the call of God always do so from some realization that they are weak, helpless and sinful, that they are in some way deficient and lacking.

Those who perceive themselves to be in this kind of condition do so in different ways and at different times and in different degrees. Thus, they respond differently. Once in a great while the call comes in a striking and dramatic fashion and results in a dramatic conversion (e.g. Saint Paul's conversion experience—*Acts 9:1–14*). But such a dramatic call is most unusual, and even in a case like this it is probably only the culmination of many previous, quieter calls. In Saint Paul's case, for example, he must have been struggling with himself, pondering over the words and example of Saint Stephen, the first Christian martyr, whose death Paul had witnessed *(Acts 7:54–60, 8:1–3)*.

Questions
● What *obstacles* are we apt to encounter which may prevent us from hearing the call of God to conversion?
● What can we do to *overcome* these obstacles?

Obstacles

We are apt to encounter the following obstacles:

1. *Lack of recognition.* The call will seldom be loud and clear and we can fail to notice it. Often we need the help of a guide in order to be able to discern the call and see it for what it is.

2. *Confusion and distraction.* We may be so busy about many things that we do not take the time to reflect upon and sort out what is happening in our life.

3. *Living in the past.* If we judge everything by what was done in the past we may miss something new that is happening to us *now.*

4. *Living in the future.* We can fail to hear the call that is being given *now* because we are busy daydreaming about how things might be *someday,* how God might call us in the future.

5. *False expectations.* If we expect a dramatic event we may miss the call which God is giving in a quiet way through ordinary happenings, in the daily events of our life.

In addition, there are certain fears which can be obstacles:

1. *Fear of failure.* "I can't do it. I wouldn't make it."

2. *Fear of destruction.* "If I follow this out I'll be no longer myself. I'll become an oddball, a 'holy Joe.' I'll be *different.* I'll no longer be *myself."*

3. *Fear of rejection.* "The people who are important to me and significant in my life will no longer accept me. I'll be *alone."*

4. *Fear of pain.* "This will be hard. It will hurt. It will cost me a great deal."

Overcoming Obstacles

We can strive to overcome obstacles such as these by trying to be the following:

1. Attentive—aware of what is happening to us.

2. Discerning—looking for hitherto unnoticed or unrealized possibilities of things we might do for others, things that are possible for us to do, not grand solutions that are beyond our reach.

3. Responsible—basing what decisions for action we arrive at on the consequences we can see for ourselves and for others in both short term and long term benefits.

4. Reasonable—unafraid to reject what we think probably will not work at this time and settle on doing what seems reasonable to us here and now.

5. Open—realizing that God's call becomes clearer and more embracing with time and requires openness and readiness to change little by little.

6. Willing to take risks—being willing to plunge in when, after all, we haven't had a call from God so obvious and clear that we couldn't mistake it.

7. Aware of God's willingness to help us and our need to pray. As we listen to God, we discover means and solutions we had not noticed before, and as we pray we find strength and courage and the ability to go ahead and persevere. As we pray with others, we gain strength and support from them, the kind of human support which God provides through other people.

THE CHRISTIAN COMMUNITY

The call of God to conversion is given to each individual as it was to John and Andrew. But the call given to each individual is not merely an invitation to closer intimacy with God for that individual. It is always God's intention that the individual achieve that intimacy and the growth it entails within the context of a community. This notion does not appeal to some people. They would much prefer to deal with God privately, praying to him and relating to him entirely on their own, without the cumbersome paraphernalia of a church and with all the formalism and legal matters that are inevitable in such institutions.

The call to a new way of life, especially when it is a call to change one's life drastically, is a call to join other like-minded people who will share with, guide, and support the one who is called. When a person answers God's call to a new way of living, that person will find that many old friends are no longer comfortable or supportive. In fact, the person may find that old friends try to entice one back to the "old" way of life. It is only by joining people who try to live the "new" way that a person can persevere in and fully live out the "new" way of life.

God created the human race as a family and each person as a member of that family. In that family he has called certain people to a special unity—a special identity—in order to be a sign to all people that God loves the human race and that he wishes all people to live in peace and unity. Therefore, his call to the individual involves a call to become a member of this special people which God began to form about four thousand years ago.

The Old Testament is a record of God's continuing and progressive community-building among people. God called Abraham not merely in an expression of love for an individual but in order to begin his plan for a whole people who would be God's chosen people. He raised up prophets among those people in order to keep them united and faithful to him and to their mission. Jesus called the apostles and formed them into a group, or *college*. He preached love and unity to his followers and brought them together into a community. He prayed that the love and unity among them might reflect the union between himself and the Father. He sent the Spirit to enhance and perfect community among his followers.

However much one might wish to avoid involvement with a community and the inevitable institutionalizing which human community always entails, one cannot really do so. It is such a community that gave us the Old and the New Testaments. As Christians, we are heirs to the community of God's people in the Old Testament. And were it not for the community which was formed by the followers of Jesus we would never have heard of him except for a mere mention in the book of an ancient historian.

In fact, so involved is God in the matter of community that it is true and necessary to say that the call he gives— the summons to growth—is given not only to individuals who will become members of a community but also to the community itself. The call to individuals is a call not only to change their individual ways but also to join with other like-minded people and to respond to God as a group as well as individually. And the process of conversion goes on not only in the individuals but also within the community of people who are constantly and continually being called as a community, to be faithful to God and to their mission.

PERSONAL PROFILE

The questions and exercises in the Personal Profile are an integral part of *Becoming Catholic*. They help us look into our *real* goals, our *real* beliefs, our *basic* assumptions about life. They are a tool to help us paint for ourselves a picture of ourselves, a self-portrait which will help us see ourselves from different angles, in different moods, thinking, feeling, acting and reacting day by day under different circumstances. The Personal Profile is something we build by ourselves, for ourselves, not for purposes of entertainment or nostalgia, but for true understanding and self-knowledge.

The Personal Profile will help us sort out our thoughts and feelings on important questions, review them in the light of our experience and bring them together in harmony with new insights we may have gained from our study of and dialogue about the Gospel.

There are three parts to the Personal Profile:
1. A *Review* of the preceding section.
2. *Prayer*—selections of Scripture passages related to the theme of the section which can serve as the basis of prayer during the interval between the sessions.
3. A *Preview* to prepare for the following section.
You may wish to keep your Personal Profile very private. In that case write the answers in a personal notebook or in a journal-type book which you can keep in a safe place.

If you are not concerned that someone might read what you have written, it may be more convenient to jot down the answers to the *Review* and *Preview* section right in this book.

Review

One time in the past when I heard a call from God was when

_____

_____

(Name a person, an event, an experience which you felt was a call from God to a new and better life.)

I received help in answering that call from _____

_____

(Be specific as to the kind of help and who offered it.)

The difficulty I had in answering that call was _____

_____

(Be as specific as possible as to the difficulties you experienced in responding to the call.)

At this time in my life I think I hear God calling me

From _____ to _____

From _____ to _____

From _____ to _____

(Try to be specific as to the things you hear God calling you to change in your life.)

The help I would anticipate from the group involved in *Becoming Catholic* (or in going through the book by myself)

is _____

_____

Prayer

The Scripture selections indicated are intended to help you in your prayer. Feel free to use them any way that helps you pray. However, various ways will be suggested throughout the book on how to use Scripture as a basis for prayer. Each passage can be used for at least one period of prayer. You need not spend a long time reflecting and praying on these passages.

Sacred Scripture has numerous accounts of God calling, summoning, people to live in trust. He calls people directly—he elects them. He calls them indirectly—he comes to them through other people. Each election entails a mission and each person who is elected can experience the mystery of God's call.

One way to experience the power of these passages, to enter into the Scriptures, is to put yourself in the place of the main character and talk to God about how you feel and think as you realize that he is calling you.

● *Genesis 12:1–9.* Abraham's call and mission from God and his response to that call.

● *Exodus 3:4–14.* The call of Moses and his response to that call and to the mission given him.

● *Luke 1:26–38.* The call of Mary and her response to God's election and mission.

● *Mark 2:13–17.* The call of Levi by Jesus and the response of Levi to that call and mission.

Preview

The Preview is intended to help you get in touch with your experiences of the material in the next section. It will help you surface your *real* feelings and thoughts on the subject. Be as honest as you can even though you find that what you feel and think is not in line with what you think you are expected to feel and think. There are no right or wrong answers in these exercises. There are merely YOUR answers and thoughts and feelings.

The next section is about the God who calls, the God who is presented in Scripture. This God has many faces. Which of his faces are you most comfortable with? On the line between the contrasting aspects of God mark with an X the spot where you feel most comfortable.

A stern judgmental God			A kindly loving God
A God controlling the world and people's lives from without			A God living and acting within people and events, cooperating with them
A God of might and majesty desirous of our obedience and worship			A God who is a father whom we can address by the endearing term of *Daddy*

A God who becomes angry when people sin			A God who never becomes angry with his children and never stops loving them no matter what they do
A God described by his many attributes such as all powerful, all merciful, etc.			A God as seen in his actions in the lives of people
A God who never changes			A God who seems to change
A God whom we can never really understand			A God whom we can understand and describe
A God who is Father			A God who is Mother

2

The God Who Calls

Abram was a prosperous man. He owned large flocks of goats and sheep. His life was pleasant and uneventful. In fact, it was pleasantly uneventful. He lived secure in a fertile land surrounded by family, relatives, and friends. All indications were that he would live to a happy old age in these familiar, safe, and comfortable circumstances.

But the indications were wrong. Abram heard a call—a call from God. The Book of Genesis puts it simply and starkly. "The Lord said to Abram, 'Go from your country and your kindred and your father's house to the land that I will show you' " *(Genesis 12:1)*.

Who was this God who was calling Abram? He told Abram nothing about himself, not even His name. He asked a great deal—that Abram uproot himself from all that was comfortable and familiar to go off into the unknown. He promised a great deal in return—a land, a country, and descendants as numerous as the stars of the heavens. But these were promises not yet realities. Still, there was one thing about this God who was calling that, even at this point, was clear. He cared. He was concerned about Abram and his future. He came unbidden and unsought into Abram's life. He obviously had Abram's interests at heart. What he asked of Abram was a response of faith. And Abram gave that response, fully and whole-heartedly. The Book of Genesis puts it quite simply: "So Abram went, as the Lord had told him" *(Genesis 12:1–9)*.

Moses, too, was living in safe and comfortable circumstances. His was a peaceful life in the desert. As an Israelite, even though he had fled from Egypt where his people lived in bondage, he knew dimly of this God who had called Abram, changed his name to Abraham and given him great promises. But beyond that Moses knew very little of this God.

Then suddenly, just as suddenly as the call had come to Abraham, it came to Moses. This time it was accompanied by a strange phenomenon—a burning bush. From the bush God spoke to Moses. Again it was a summons, "Come, I will send you to Pharaoh that you may bring forth my people, the sons of Israel, out of Egypt." But now this God was not entirely unknown. He announced himself, "I am the God of your fathers, the God of Abraham, Isaac, and Jacob." When Moses protested that he did not know God's name, God told him his name, Yahweh. He showed his caring and protective power by enabling Moses to overcome the stubbornness of Pharaoh and by destroying the Egyptian army that came in pursuit of the departing Israelites. And, most of all, he showed by his continuous care and concern for Moses and his people, that he was a God of love and compassion.

Throughout the long period during which the Israelites lived as nomads in the desert, this God continued to summon them, day by day, leading them from oasis to oasis, communicating with them through Moses. And the people came to know that God who had chosen them as the God who cared for them and loved them as the "apple of his eye." *(Exodus 3:1–20:21)*.

Moses and his people knew God not as a remote, impersonal force living in some inaccessible region out in the sky. No, they knew him as a God of love who took the initiative, who lived in and among his people, a God who acted personally in the lives of all his children.

This is a God who bears no resemblance to the gods of the pagans.

Other nations worshiped gods who were clearly idealizations of themselves, personifications of the forces of nature or reflections of human experience. The God of Israel is utterly unlike these pagan gods. He is no figure in a myth, no personification of a natural force. He did not emerge out of the legends of the tribe. He is not an incorporation of its ideas. He is a vital personality who intruded himself into the world of the Hebrews. He is not one national god who exists alongside of the gods of other nations. He is unique. He is, as the Israelites came to understand during their exile in Babylon, the only God, the one true God, and above all, a God who loves and cares for them.

But even at the time of Moses the people had to wrestle with a view of God which pictured him as a just judge, rewarding the good and punishing the wicked. They attributed their freedom from slavery, their victories in battle, their promised land, their very food to his merciful providence and love. But they also attributed to him their defeats in battle, their famines, their illnesses. They saw him as rewarding and punishing them in a material or external way.

Later the prophets and the reflective religious people began to see that the calamities which they suffered had a good side. These disasters brought the nation back to the observance of their convenant or pact with God. The prophets spoke of these events as signs of God's love because the prophets saw them as the means God used to bring his people back to faithfulness. Again and again God came to the rescue of his people. Each generation that abandoned the true God and violated the covenant encountered suffering and misery. And in every single case, when the people cried out to God and returned to friendship with him, he rescued them and brought them peace and prosperity.

But as the Scriptures also tell us, in books such as Job, the people were wrestling with the obvious problem posed by this view of God. They saw the suffering of good people who lived by the Law and the prosperity of people who ignored or broke the Law.

The love of God in the Old Testament seems to be restricted to one nation, the Israelites. They were God's chosen people—chosen not for any merits of their own but simply because God loved them. He sent them leaders to save them not because they deserved to be delivered from their enemies but simply because he loved them.

The reason for this exclusiveness is that the Old Testament is concerned with the religious history and experiences of this one people, the Israelites. But the Old Testament makes it clear also, that this loving and caring God does love and care for all peoples.

Abraham was a pagan who had no knowledge of the true God. Yet God called him because he loved him personally. But, more than that, God called Abraham because he loved not only the Israelites, who would be the children of Abraham, but also the whole human race, which is the ultimate heir to the promise God made to Abraham. That God is a God of all people and a God who loves all is beautifully demonstrated in the short stories about Jonah, the prophet sent to save the pagan enemies of the Israelites, and about Ruth, the Moabite ancestress of David.

When Jesus came and began to speak to the people about God, he held out to them a vision of God many of them could not accept because it seemed foreign to their tradition. The Jews stood in such awe of the Lord God that they did not pronounce the name he had given to Moses, "Yahweh," but substituted the word "Lord." Jesus spoke of God in the most intimate terms, calling him not only Father, but even calling him by the familiar and endearing term "Abba," the English equivalent of which would be "Daddy." The Jews felt that they alone were the special subjects of God's love, but Jesus said that all people who accepted the Lord in their hearts were chosen people. Moreover, the reward for faithfulness presented by Jesus was not material prosperity but inner peace and joy. It was the intimate friendship which comes from God—Father, Son, and Spirit—living in the hearts of his people. Jesus also made it clear that the physical afflictions of people were not a punishment for sins visited on them by God but part of the human situation.

When he spoke of the justice of God, it was in terms of separation from a loving Father who loves his children enough to allow them the freedom even to leave him and be separated from him. Perhaps, the most beautiful description of God given by Jesus is in the story of the Prodigal Son. The father loves the boy enough to allow him to depart without a word of reproach. He did not want his son to suffer, but he would not forcibly restrain him from wasting his life and enduring hunger and poverty. But the father's love was so great that he accepted his wayward son back with great joy, without a word of reproach when the son returned, even though he hoped for no more than a decent meal and a place to work and live *(Luke 15:11–32).*

Jesus spoke of God, his Father and our Father, as a God of infinite love, the loving creator whose eye is on the sparrow, who cares for the lilies of the field and much more for us, his own children. In parable after parable Jesus spelled out for us how much the Father loves us, how he cares for us, and how merciful and forgiving he is.

But above all Jesus showed us the Father when he showed us himself—as the friend of sinners, the one who spent his whole life in loving care for others, the one who gladly laid down his life for us, saying "There is no greater love than this." And as Jesus showed the love, compassion, and mercy he embodies, he said, "Whoever sees me sees the Father."

The picture of God presented in the Scriptures changed greatly between the time the first books were written, about 900 B.C., and the last one, about 100 A.D. Yet we find that in some way the people of all ages wrestled with the same questions. They were concerned with reconciling God's love and justice, with the proper degree of familiarity and respect and reverence, with his presence among them and his transcendent presence throughout the universe, with his power, and with their own freedom. Looking back, we can see that whenever the people did not keep these opposing tendencies in some sort of balance, they were creating a god in their own likeness rather than accepting the God who revealed himself. But when people kept these opposing tendencies in a creative tension, they gradually came to a deeper understanding and appreciation of what God was actually telling about himself.

Questions
- How do people today *envision* God and think of him?
- How does the *image* we have of God affect our life?
- Why do some people find it *difficult* to think of God as a loving God?

Envisioning God

Everyone has his or her own way of envisioning God. People may use the same words in speaking of God, but each person has an idea of God which has evolved from what has been taught, seen, heard, experienced, and reflected on during that person's life.

Few deny that some sort of intelligent force brought the world into existence, but many conclude that this force, power, being, or whatever has no care or concern for the world, and certainly no interest in individuals. Many others think of God as a power or force with benign intentions and interest which is operative in the world but avoid terms such as "father" and "lord" and even pronouns such as "he" or "she," on the grounds that such terms cause us to think of God as some sort of superman who lives in the sky. Some think of God as the Ground of Being—an all-powerful and loving Presence from which all things come and in which they live and act and have their being.

Many people derive their notion of God from the Bible. Some dwell on God as they remember him from Old Testament stories—a God who is loving and just at the same time, moved to anger, quick to punish, demanding to be placated, but also forgiving and capable of being affected by our prayers. Many others dwell more on the picture of God that Jesus presents, that of a loving Father, all powerful, loving, caring, forgiving, but also just. Most adult Christians realize that even when Jesus speaks of God as Father he is doing what we all do, speaking of God as if he had human qualities and characteristics, since this is really the only way we can speak of him. They realize that God is a spirit, but still picture him in their imagination as some sort of super-human human being.

Some people put more emphasis on God's justice than on his love. Others emphasize the love of God and underplay the idea of justice. Some stress God's power and control over even the most minute details of life. Others see God as leaving man free to work out his life and destiny and explore and develop the world.

Image of God—Its Effect

The image of God people have will dictate how they relate to God, to life, and to other people. One whose image of God is that of an impersonal, uncaring force will have a totally secular view of life. Those who see God as strict, stern, exacting, and punishing may either reject him as too unpleasant to deal with or live in constant fear of offending him and be at constant pains to placate him. Such people often adopt a stern, unmerciful, and intolerant attitude to-wards others.

On the other hand, the New Testament and the lives of people who truly believe in a loving God show that this view of God leads to inner peace and joy. It inspires people to share the Good News with others. It frees people from fear and neurotic guilt, and it gives them hope when they experience healthy guilt because of their sins. It helps them to be tolerant of people who hold opinions other than theirs, and it especially motivates them to reach out in love to their less fortunate brothers and sisters.

A person who truly believes that God loves all people will try to do something about at least one of the many social problems facing the world today. St. John in his first epistle describes the life of one who loves God. The focal point of this love is love and service to others.

The man who claims to be in light, hating his brother all the while, is in darkness even now. The man who continues in the light is the one who loves his brother. . . . I ask you, how can God's love survive in a man who has enough of this world's goods yet closes his heart to his brother when he sees him in need. If anyone says, "My love is fixed on God," yet hates his brother, he is a liar. One who has no love for the brother he has seen cannot love the God he has not seen.

(1 John 2:9–10, 3:17, 4:20)

Jesus presented God as our loving Father. He used the word "abba," the closest English equivalent of which would be "daddy." And yet many people face real problems in growing in their image of God and in responding to him as Jesus presented him.

1. Just as ancient cultures made their gods in their own image and likeness, so too people now tend to make God in their own image and likeness. If we tend to be strict disciplinarians, letter of the law people, quick to condemn and slow to praise, we see God in somewhat the same way.

We ourselves find it very difficult to love everyone, especially people who seem to us to be unlovable. We find it hard, too, to forgive those who hurt us. Therefore, we have difficulty imagining that anyone, even God, can be all loving and all forgiving.

Morever, we tend to be vindictive. We want to see wrongdoers punished. We naturally feel a satisfaction in thinking that even though we can't punish those we would like to, at least God will give them what they deserve.

We tend, falsely, to think that we are deserving of rewards because we have denied ourselves pleasures and tried to lead good lives. We are like the men in Christ's parable, those who worked all day and resented being paid no more than those hired at the last minute. We may feel cheated to think that others might get away with things we were so virtuous as to have avoided. Therefore, although we may be reluctant to admit it to ourselves, we might favor the idea of a God who is vindictive, at least where others are concerned.

Finally, since in our experience we have never known anyone who is completely loving and infinitely merciful, we cannot imagine such a being.

2. Some people have such a poor self-image that they feel that no one, not even God, can love them. They cannot accept the good news that God does love them and that he does see good in them.

3. People very early identify God with their parents, who are authority figures. Those with kind and loving parents who showed affection are apt to have a picture of God as a loving and merciful Father. Those whose parents were stern, threatening, and quick to punish are apt to picture God as a strict and exacting judge. The way God was presented in childhood has a strong influence on the way people come to feel about him even as adults. When children are told to fear a God who is always watching them even when no one else is and is keeping score and waiting to punish them for every transgression, they tend to carry this impression over into adult life. On the other hand, when children are raised with the idea of a merciful God who loves and understands them and wills only their welfare and their happiness, they tend to have a notion of God as loving Father.

4. Many people merely repeat the words others have spoken about God. They have not reflected on their words or tried to make them their own. They have not reflected on their own experience to see whether the words make sense to them.

5. Some people do not advance beyond the idea of the all-powerful, magician type God which is common among and proper to small children. Such people expect God to run things, to overcome evil, in reality to restrict the freedom of people. When God does not work the miracles they want, they reject him, put him aside as a childish fantasy with no relevance to their lives.

6. Others are so taken by the majesty and power of God that they have a difficult time seeing him as a personal God, interested in them. They see God rather as a force, a power, not one who is really interested in any human being.

7. Other people form false and misleading ideas about God from observing some so-called religious people who are self-righteous, unforgiving, exclusive, or judgmental. They do not see the God Jesus spoke of when they observe some of those who profess to be followers of Jesus.

Questions

● Might the *stress on the mercy and love* of God give people the idea that they can flaunt the commandments and do anything they want and get away with it?

● What can we do to *grow* in our way of seeing God and to bring our image of God more in line with the image Jesus presents?

● How does God *help* us to come to know him as a loving Father?

Stress on Mercy and Love

Presenting God as a God of love and putting stress on his mercy and forgiveness might cause some people to think that one can flaunt the commandments—do whatever you want and get away with it. It might do so for those whose sole reason for being moral is fear of punishment. But according to the Scriptures, that type of "childish morality" is of no avail to a person anyway. As St. Paul says, "If I have not love, I am nothing." The whole thrust of the Christian message is that we live and act according to adult Christian moral standards out of love for God and love for one another. One cannot imagine Mary Magdalene, after her encounter with the love of Jesus, resolving to lead a chaste life

27

in the future because she feared that Jesus would punish her if she did not. Nor can we imagine that Zaccheus, the tax collector, would have reformed his life for such a motive. Surely, they and all the other sinners who came to know Jesus reformed their lives because they wanted to measure up to and in some way return the love Jesus and the Father had for them.

This is not to say that sinners "get away" with anything. Such an idea might be founded on the assumption that a life of sin is fun and one of virtue is a grim thing which is of value only because there will be a reward in the next life. Sin has consequences, if not in this life, then in eternity. One who closes oneself off from love—love of God and love of others—moves more and more into self-imposed damnation. Hell is a reality that Jesus warned us about. It is the ultimate consequence of unrepented sin. In urging us to live a life of love, free from sin, Jesus is telling us how to be happy—not only in the next world but even, as far as possible, in this life. It may be an oversimplification to say that virtue is its own reward and vice its own punishment. But it is true that sin has a way of catching up with the sinner. On the other hand, Jesus holds out to us a life of love which is a life of adults striving to rise above our sinfulness and live as he did.

A good motto for all might be that of St. Teresa, who often said that she wanted always to act out of love of God but prayed that if ever her love wasn't strong enough the fear of hell would keep her from sinning.

Growth

We can do several things to grow in our way of seeing God and to bring it more closely in line with the image of God presented by Jesus.

1. We can look at all the gifts each of us has and realize that we are good and lovable just because we are who we are. We can strive to see the good in others and to love and serve others, not because they necessarily deserve our love, but because they are basically good, even though they may sometimes act in ways destructive to others and themselves. We can also open ourselves to others, and by accepting love we will come to a clearer realization of the love God has for us.

The same is true of forgiveness. The more we forgive and accept forgiveness, the more we will realize the meaning of God's mercy and forgiveness.

The more we look into ourselves and into the lives of others and see how *our* own decisions and actions have brought suffering into our lives and the less we blame others or circumstances for our problems, the clearer will become our realization of the meaning of God's justice.

2. It is also helpful to share and compare our ideas and experiences of God with those of others who have different ideas and experiences. We can especially study what the mystics and saints have said about God. Through such discussion and study we may discover that some of our ideas are still rather immature and childish.

If we reach out to God by trying to live a life guided by the principles and example of Jesus, if we seek what others have found in God, especially by reflecting on Scripture and the writings of the great mystics, God will respond and make himself known to us as he actually is.

How God Helps Us

God does not leave us on our own. He is always present, always trying to bring us to himself—always trying to help us know him better and relate to him more intimately. His help comes to us in many ways, including the following:

- Through love we experience from other people.
- Through the good things that happen in our lives which some ascribe to luck, others to providence.
- Through the suffering and misfortunes which help us to grow in a way we would never have grown if they had not occurred.

29

- Through history (e.g., Scriptures and the history of Christian community) in which we can see God acting to show his love and care.
- Through his active presence within us, which at special times we are aware of in a deep and profound way.

THE CHRISTIAN COMMUNITY

The Christian community has its roots in the Old Testament. For a deeper understanding of the Christian community, therefore, and an appreciation of its continuing growth and development, we need some understanding of the growth and development of God's people in the Old Testament.

In the earliest years the Hebrew people had only a vague idea of this God they were convinced was their special God and protector. He was a remote deity who had called Abraham, given him a vision and a destiny and then, mysteriously, inexplicably retreated into silence. Then, when he reasserted himself in the dramatic events of the Exodus, these people, now known as Israelites, saw this God as a warrior-god who had made a special covenant with them. They did not see him as the only god at first. He was simply *their* god, and the covenant he had made with them was for them, even though its promises held out hope for benefits for all people through them.

As the people of Israel grew and developed through the centuries, so did their understanding of their God. It was only after what looked like the end of the world for them when they were destroyed as a nation and led off into exile in a pagan land that the Israelites came to the fuller understanding of God. When they returned from exile these people of God, now known as the Jewish people, were deeply convinced that this God—their God—was the only God, that he was present everywhere, that he was all powerful, that he was a god of love who cared for all humankind. Even with this deeper understanding of God, the Israelites continued to regard him in a special way as theirs and his love and concern for the rest of the world as secondary.

The earliest Christian community in Jerusalem was a community within a community. It was part of the Jewish community. It shared its beliefs, it continued to join in the worship of the temple and the synagogue. But very soon the community of Christians began to realize that God was calling them to a broader vision, a larger destiny. They grew in their understanding of God as the Father of Jesus who loved the world with an all-inclusive, universal love and who was calling them to extend the knowledge and love of him to the world by preaching Christ and his message to all mankind.

The Christian community has had its own growth and development, just as did the Jewish community from which it came. There was the militant stand against paganism. Christians could discern nothing good in any of the beliefs or practices of the pagans. When they were in a position to do so they destroyed everything that smacked of paganism. What they could not destroy they baptized and assimilated. As the Church moved out into the world of Greece and Rome, it formulated its creed in terms of Greek philosophy and organized itself along the lines of the Roman legal system. The Christian community always reflected the age and culture in which it found itself. As it grew and developed, it acted and reacted to that culture. It made use of the science and learning of each age, with all the virtues and all the limitations of that science and learning. Christians, divided from one another by the Eastern Schism and by the Protestant Reformation, were hostile towards one another as they had been against the pagans in an earlier age. Various Christian bodies made claim to being the best, the truest, the most authentic expression of Christianity. The Roman Catholic Church took the strongest position, declaring that other dissenting Christian bodies were heretics and not part of the true Church.

The growth of the Christian community has been marked, then, by a constant succession of struggles, the struggles of weak, sinful human beings seeking to understand themselves, God, and the message of Jesus and to relate all this to their lives, their mission, and their destiny.

The signs of growth are here today, along with and sometimes identical with the struggles that are a part of growth. Intellectual speculation about God and life, a characteristic of the Greek philosophical and theological approach, has been replaced by a more biblical approach. The result is a growing openness to one another among Christian bodies and churches. Communities of Christians, although by no means united, are more prone to listen to one another, learn from one another, share with one another, and even to acknowledge that each has a place within the Church of Jesus Christ. The Roman Catholic Church now officially recognizes that the various Christian churches and denominations are all part of the Church in the wider sense of that term. Christians are becoming more aware of their need for one another—for a sharing of the various traditions and communions which have been growing within the Christian church for centuries. And within the Christian communities and in the larger Christian community throughout the world there is a constant struggle to keep and cherish the wisdom of the past and to find its meaning in the present.

PERSONAL PROFILE

In your Personal Profile it is not necessary to worry about correct spelling or grammar. Record what you think and feel in words, phrases, complete sentences, prose, poetry. The Profile is for you to help yourself, and writing things down helps to clarify what you think and feel.

Review

Our relationship to God is in the here and now. Memories of how I knew and experienced him in the past give me roots and a frame of reference. Hopes for the way I will know and experience him in the future give me a sense of direction. But the past is past and the future has not arrived. I live with God only in the here and now. The way I knew him in the past may not be the way I know him now nor the way I hope to know him in the future. Think about how you know and feel about God right now. Write down adjectives and phrases which describe your feelings about him rather than your ideas about him. Consult your feelings whether they be positive or negative. Even the absence of feelings about him is important.

_____

_____

_____

_____

_____

_____

_____

Next try to describe in a few words the place you feel God has in your life and your relationship to him.

_____

_____

_____

_____

_____

_____

Prayer

There are many images of God in Scripture. The images we have of him will direct the way we pray. Many of the Scripture images convey the picture of God as "reaching out," offering and extending his love, his creative healing to each one of us. We can make each of the following passages the basis for prayer by focusing our attention on God as one who is reaching out to help us. After we read the passage and reflect on how God is touching our lives, we can speak to him about how we feel about the joy, sorrow, fear, or anger we have. We can speak about our needs and our gratitude for his gifts.

● God the *potter*, who firmly yet gently molds people into his own image *(Genesis 2:4–7* and *Jeremiah 18:1–9)*.

● God the *surgeon*, who heals the sick and suffering *(Genesis 2:18–22, Deuteronomy 21:4–9*, and *Deuteronomy 30:15–20, Psalm 6:1–6)*.

● God the *shield*, the *rock*, the *fortress*, the *defender*, who reaches out and protects people *(Genesis 15:1–6, Psalm 18:1–4*, and *Psalm 31:1–9)*.

● God the *shepherd* and *host* who cares for his people and guests *(Psalm 23:1–4* and *5–6, Psalm 36:6–10*, and *Matthew 18:10–14)*.

Preview

Jesus told a story about a farmer who went out to plant in his field. Some of the seed fell on a footpath and never took root. Some fell on infertile soil or among thorns, took root but quickly died. Some fell on good ground and yielded a good harvest *(Matthew 13:4–9)*. The seed is the word of God. We are the ground. In all of us there are patches of good soil and patches of hardened or infertile soil. In column 1, write the personal qualities you have as well as the people and circumstances of your life which you think make you good "soil" to receive the call of God. In column 2, write your personal qualities and the people and circumstances in your life which you think harden you so that you do not hear the call of God or give it a chance to grow.

1. Good Soil   **2. Hardened Soil**

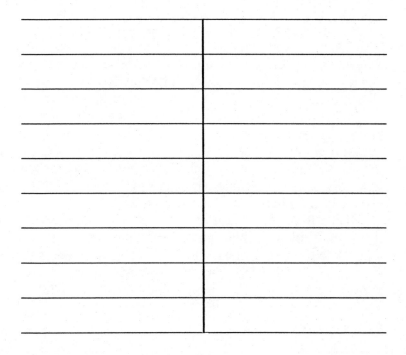

3

Our Response to God's Call

The road was a wide grayish-yellow ribbon snaking its way to Damascus under the blazing sun. It was mid-day. There was not a single cloud in the sky to shield the little band of travelers from the heat as they trudged along the dusty road. But the heat and the dust were no real deterrent to the leader of the group. The set of his jaw, the gleam in his eye, the firmness of his step, all indicated that he was a man of purpose, a man with a mission he was impatient to accomplish. And, indeed this man was such a man. He was Saul, a devout follower of the Law, a man whose religious zeal had driven him to the point where he had become a sort of vigilante, bent on ferreting out and throwing into prison the followers of this Jesus of Nazareth. And this was the purpose of his journey to Damascus. He took reassurance from the weight of the leather pouch that hung from his shoulder. In it were the official papers authorizing him to arrest these followers of the Nazarene who were even now living and spreading their heresy in Damascus.

Then it came—a flash of lightning that threw Saul to the ground, blinding him, and leaving him trembling with fear. Then the voice, which only Saul heard, speaking those strange words, "Saul, Saul, why do you persecute me?" Even in his terror Saul was able to blurt out a question: "Who are you?" And the answer came, "I am Jesus, the one you are persecuting."

This shattering encounter was the call that was to transform Saul into Paul, the great apostle of Jesus. The call came suddenly and miraculously. Saul's response was immediate, too. But the transformation would be a slow, gradual, difficult process. It was not a matter of rising, dusting himself off, taking a new name and setting out to be an apostle of Christ. For Paul, it meant a period of blindness, being led by others to a man who would teach him day by day. Then would come a long period of prayer and solitude in the desert. After that, a pilgrimage to Jerusalem to meet with Peter and the others and gain their confidence and acceptance *(Galatians 1:15–19)*. Then a day-by-day living as a missionary, wrestling with himself and the ever-occurring problems that would arise from people and circumstances *(2 Corinthians 11:26–28)*.

But the initial response of Paul was the beginning. It was a response of faith. It was saying "yes" to this Jesus who was calling him—a surrender to what Paul could not even guess at the time. And the slow, gradual, day-by-day living out of that first response was a series of acts of faith, a daily living of the faith that came to Paul as he responded to the call.

This tremendous conversion experience colored the whole life of the apostle Paul. The response he gave to the call of Jesus was the dominant note in all his preaching and writing. It was faith, deep, personal faith in Jesus Christ. And this faith was not a matter of mere assent of the mind and expressions given in words. It changed Paul's way of thinking and acting day by day to such an extent that he was able to say, "The life I live now is not my own; Christ is living in me. I still live my human life, but it is a life of faith in the Son of God, who loved me and gave himself for me" *(Galatians 2:20)*.

This response of faith is the response of everyone who answers the call of Jesus to conversion, to growth, to further growth. It is a response that shows itself in a life like that of Jesus. This does not mean that one begins to *do* the things Jesus did. This would be mere external imitation—doing

37

"holy things" all day without ever becoming holy. Rather, it means making one's own the principles by which Jesus lived and living according to them, seeking to do the will of God in all things and living a life of love of and service to others.

Questions
- What kind of response is to be hoped for when one receives the call to conversion?
- What happens in a person's life when that person says a genuine "yes" to God's call?
- What are the dispositions we need in order to say "yes" to God's call?

Hoped for Response

The ideal response would be that of Mary, "I am the servant of the Lord. Let it be done to me as you say" *(Luke 1:38)*.

Actually, many people respond slowly, bit by bit, sometimes with some reluctance. For some, the first response is to wrestle with the call, to fight it for a time before making a firm decision to follow it up. There will often be some vacillation and some setbacks. The process of conversion is a life journey, an ongoing process, not an act or a series of isolated acts.

What Happens in One's Life

When a person says a genuine "yes" to God's call, his or her way of acting and living begins to change. A person's beliefs also change. The person begins to change his or her way of looking at and explaining life, religious experiences, etc. Even if the person's professed beliefs do not change, actual beliefs do, because the *professed* beliefs are now interiorized and have become the person's *actual* beliefs.

Dispositions

In order to respond to God's call we need to have certain qualities.

1. Openness to change. We need to be willing to explore the need and the possibility of change in the way we see and relate to God, in the way we look at and live life, and in what we value most highly in our lives.

2. Courage. We have to be willing to embrace the unknown; to put our lives into the hands of God, even though we do not know where he might be leading us; to give up familiar, safe, and comfortable ways of thinking and acting; to adopt new and untried ways of being and acting.

3. Attentiveness. God's call usually is gentle, like an evening breeze, and it requires that we try to be sensitive to it when it is given. We need to be attentive to the circumstances of our lives in order to hear what God is saying to us.

4. Reflectiveness. When we think we have heard God call and have said "yes" to him, we need to think over and ponder our faith experience in order to become more and more sensitive to God's presence and activity in our lives.

As we reflect, we begin to *understand* what is happening. We begin to *sort out and clarify* how we feel and think about God and Christ. Then we become more able to articulate these thoughts and feelings and express them both in what we believe (our beliefs) and in what we do (our actions), which are influenced by our beliefs.

5. Honesty. We need to be able to face ourselves honestly, to accept the facts about where we are, what we are, and what we have done.

6. Perseverance. We need to keep following the way we perceive that God is showing us, in spite of difficulties and discouragements and the temptation to give up.

Questions
● What are the difficulties we are apt to encounter in our effort to hear and respond to the call of God?
● How does God help us to face these difficulties?

Difficulties

We are apt to encounter two main types of difficulties—those which come from within ourselves and those which come from the culture in which we live.

From within. We have to struggle with *inertia,* our tendency to stay with what we know, with what seems "safer" and more "secure," with the "tried and true" rather than take a chance on the unknown. Often, people do not hear the call of God because changing their way of life, sometimes a sinful way, seems to be too hard, seems to demand too much.

We have to struggle with *fear.* Whenever we are called to move into the unknown, a certain amount of fear is present. This fear takes many forms: fear of rejection, loss of freedom, destruction of one's personhood, fear of suffering, fear of loneliness, etc.

We have to struggle with *impulsiveness.* In our eagerness to find God we could run off hither and yon, following each new fad or movement without sufficient reflection on and discernment of the presence of God in what we take to be a call from him.

Besides these general difficulties, each of us may find we have personal, unique problems arising from our life experiences, which may make it difficult to hear God: physical illness, emotional or physical fatigue, poor self-image, lack of trust in God, fear of authority, a desire to remain childish and dependent on others rather than take hold of our own lives, etc.

From without. We face problems from our culture which play down maturity and personal responsibility and strive to keep us outer-directed (motivated by fads, fashions, current modes of behavior, commercials on T.V., radio, etc.) rather than inner-directed (motivated by principles we have digested and assented to and high ideals that are really our own). The culture in which we live urges us to conform, to be like everyone else, to value size rather than quality, success rather than integrity. It appeals to and fosters childish appetites and tries to get us to depend more and more on gadgets. It discourages quiet, reflective, and independent thought as well as open, frank discussion and evaluation.

How God Helps Us

When we read the Scriptures we see how God helps people around these difficulties. He sends not only other people but even his very Spirit to help those who are open to his call.

He sent the prophets to make his will clear and to encourage and help people turn once again to the covenant. He sent Jesus. Jesus sent his disciples to encourage people to overcome their fear, inertia, impulsiveness, and sinfulness and to become open and accepting. Both the prophets and followers of Jesus formed communities which supported people in their efforts to say "yes" to God.

But Scripture also shows that God works in the inner recesses of the human heart through his Spirit, through his own presence. He inspires, encourages, clarifies, motivates, and helps in a mysterious way deep in a person's being.

God acts today, both in each person as an individual and in society, as he did in the past to enable us to discover how we can grow and become the whole person he wants us to be.

Questions

- What is the process one goes through who has said "yes" to God's call to conversion?
- How does this process affect the way a person believes?
- Is there a conflict between the personal beliefs and convictions one comes to have and those of the Church?

The Process

The first step in the process is some sort of experience of God. This is not a dramatic, soul-shaking sort of thing, but an "ah ha!" experience. "Why, of course, this is the way it is or the way it ought to be!"

One who has had such an "ah ha!" experience naturally reflects on its meaning and comes to some conclusions about it. These conclusions are statements about the meaning of the experience. "I am convinced that God is real, present and active, that God cares for me." In theological terms, such conclusions or statements are called *beliefs*. If they are real and firmly held, these beliefs have an influence on the person's life. New ways of thinking and acting resulting from these beliefs give rise to subsequent "ah ha!" experiences. And so the process goes on.

The Process and Personal Beliefs

Everyone has some sorts of experiences which are associated with God and religion. Some people will be more reflective about these experiences than others. Some people will interpret their experiences in a negative way and draw negative conclusions. People who interpret their experience in a positive way will reflect on what has happened and try to formulate a statement or a belief about it. They usually get help in this process by sharing the experience and their reflections

42

with others to find out whether they have had similar experiences and how they have interpreted them. Those others, most often, are a community, a *church,* which has formulated a set of beliefs from the experiences its members have had throughout the centuries.

By this sharing, the experiences and beliefs of individuals gradually feed into the beliefs and doctrines of the community. The beliefs and doctrines of the community help the individual understand, grasp, and express what has happened to him or her.

Some few people "go it alone." They formulate their own beliefs by themselves, relying on their own reason to tell them what is true. They do not feel that they need any community or church. The majority of people, however, turn to a church for help.

This process of *reflecting* means that people will form strong *personal* beliefs only about those things which are personally important to them. In matters which are not important or with which they have had no experience or reason to question, they will accept the beliefs of the community without too much reflection or question.

The process of reflecting on one's experience in the light of the beliefs of a community or church can have several consequences. The person's personal beliefs can be one of the following.

1. Totally in accord with those of the community.

2. More or less in accord with those of the community.

3. Quite different from those of the community.

People whose beliefs on points important to them differ completely or very substantially from those of the community usually leave the community. People whose beliefs differ somewhat have a personal religion which they profess and follow within the context of an institutional religion.

Questions
- What is the difference between the religion of an individual and the religion of a community of faith—the religion of the Church?
- How do the religion of the individual and of the community complement one another?
- What is the process by which a person brings together his or her own personal religious beliefs and those of the Church?

Individual and Institutional Faith

The religion of a faith community or church encompasses the faith experiences, the beliefs and doctrines, the moral code, and the ritual or practices of the group. It is more universal than the religion of an individual because it flows from the experiences of many people who have lived in different ages and cultures. It contains a fullness and variety of expression that an individual cannot achieve. It is usually expressed in the life of the community and in its official documents such as creeds, books of worship, and official teachings.

The religion of the individual is highly personal. It does not have the universality and the fullness of the religion of the community. Each person is unique. Although an individual belongs to a church, he or she will have faith experiences which are highly personal. Each person will have a personal viewpoint and understanding of the doctrines the community professes. Each person will have private and personal preferences in the matter of ritual and religious practices. And each person ultimately is responsible for forming the conscience by which he or she lives and acts.

The religion of the community and of the individual should feed into one another. The faith and practice of a community grow in richness and depth by assimilating the religious experiences of individuals. Today, for example, the religious experiences of the charismatics or pentecostals are saying something to the churches which, when it is understood, digested and adapted, can enrich the tradition of the Church.

The individual, on the other hand, can derive from the community insights into faith, doctrine, morality and practice which would not occur to him or her. For example, when the Church holds a certain doctrine, a person who has difficulty understanding the doctrine or who has doubts about its truth needs to question his or her position and try to work through the difficulties. Often tremendous wisdom and truth are buried in seemingly unimportant practices and ideas. The teachings of the Church often indicate areas in a person's life which are in need of conversion.

A church which does not learn from the life experiences of all its members or which blindly follows the past or accepts only the experiences of one group as a norm, is not a healthy faith community.

An adult who accepts blindly and without thinking whatever a church or community tells him or her is acting in an immature and childish way. The same is true of one who rejects out of hand the Church's expression of its experience because it does not fit into his or her own experience or pre-suppositions.

The individual and the community must live in a process of dialogue, of asking questions, of engaging in discussion. It is the process by which a person shares his or her experiences and beliefs with the community and at the same time tries to learn from the experiences and beliefs of the community. A childish faith expects a simple, direct, and unequivocal answer to every question. An adult faith realizes that there are no easy answers to many questions, that many questions have more than one answer. Often enough, a question leads to an answer which leads to more questions. An adult faith is content to live with a certain amount of tension and ambiguity in the matter of the beliefs and practices of the community.

THE CHRISTIAN COMMUNITY

The Church, which is a community sharing and trying to live the same faith, is built up and strengthened by adults who have said "yes" to God's call. Large numbers of adherents may mean no more than that a church is a powerful social structure. It is the quality of the lives of the members which demonstrates whether or not a church is really a faith community.

The faith community responds to the call of God as a community in much the same way as do individuals. There have been times when the Church was characterized by a hearty response, times of great fidelity and fervor. The early days of the apostolic community in Jerusalem was one such time as the Acts of the Apostles relate. There have been many such times in history. Even at such times there have always been dissension, strife, and troubles of various kinds. And always, in good periods and bad, there is struggle, ambiguity, uncertainty as the Church wrestles with the problem of living the Gospel and applying it to the problems of each day and age.

The New Testament resulted from the efforts of the early Christian community to understand the experience of Jesus and apply it in the light of its own experiences as it moved out into the world. The community needed to analyze this experience and to express it so that others could share it and apply it to their own situation.

There was never complete unanimity. There was always some disagreement as to the meaning of this experience as well as to the way it was to be applied. Often, it was only when an idea began taking root that struck the community at large as being at variance with the faith of the community that the very expression of the faith became more clear. At such times, the community said "no" to the idea and the teaching was branded a heresy. There was even disagreement as to which books of the Bible were to be accepted as genuine and inspired. The Church had to make an official decision. But there was at the time, and there still is, disagreement over some of these books.

As the community grew, its beliefs crystallized into doctrines and were formulated into creeds. Different times brought different conditions, different problems—problems which had not had to be faced in earlier times. The Church during times of persecution faced a situation quite different from that which it faced when it became the state religion of Rome. The Church in an age of advanced technology faces problems quite different from those that it had to deal with in a simple agrarian society. The Church in a pluralistic society finds itself in a vastly different situation than the one in which it lived during the Middle Ages. The amazing development of science in modern times has presented the Church with new challenges and made new adjustments and re-evaluations necessary. At times, discoveries which at first seem to undermine basic doctrines and threaten the very foundations of the Church's faith have the effect, in the long run, of bolstering that faith by giving new, more penetrating insight into the meaning of the basic doctrines. The advances made by modern biblical science are an excellent example. At first these discoveries seemed to many as threats so serious as to undermine the very credibility of Scripture. Instead, they have served to bring about a much better understanding of the Bible.

One source of anxiety and frustration for many is the slowness with which the Church adapts itself to these and other changes. The problem is that a community of such proportions, a community with such a long history, and above all one with such awesome responsibilities must inevitably be cautious and slow to change. It is true that the official Church has sometimes been hasty in condemning and in claiming as doctrines of the faith opinions which were never more than opinions. But this sort of thing is an inevitable part of the slow and steady process of growth to which the Christian community is committed.

PERSONAL PROFILE

A good way to grow in consciousness of God's constant efforts to approach you and to reach out to you is to answer the first two questions in this profile not just for now but every day. Reflecting in this way on the events of each day will gradually help you see more clearly the many little ways—even the unpleasant ones—in which God calls you.

Review

God calls many times a day, and we can respond or fail to respond. Think back over the day. Write down the ways in which you see that God called you or spoke to you today. How did you respond? What qualities helped you respond or kept you from responding?

1. Today, I heard God's call _____

_____

_____

2. I answered that call by _____

_____

_____

3. I see that in answering (or ignoring) that call, I was

_____

_____

Prayer

In sacred Scripture we can discover much about important questions like, "Who am I? What am I to do? How can I celebrate and take delight in what I am and what I do?" Read the following passages. Take one or two words out of each passage which tells you *who you are*. Reflect on how you feel about applying those words to yourself. Write your feelings next to the words. When you have finished, converse with God about who you are.

	Who I am	My feelings about it
Genesis 1:27–31	_____	_____
		_____
Deuteronomy 26:16–19	_____	_____
		_____
Isaiah 43:1–8	_____	_____
		_____
Isaiah 44:21–31	_____	_____
		_____
Psalm 131:1–3	_____	_____
		_____

Read the following passages to discover *what you are to do*. Write a word or two from each passage and write how you feel about doing that. Then talk to God about what you have written.

	What I am to do	How I feel about it
Exodus 19:3–8	_____	_____
		_____
Exodus 20:1–17	_____	_____
		_____
Deuteronomy 6:4–9	_____	_____
		_____
Psalm 149:1–6	_____	_____
		_____

Read the following passages to see how to *celebrate who you are and what you do*. Pick out the key word or words in each passage. Write how you feel about them and then praise and thank God for his goodness to you.

	I celebrate by	How I feel
Psalm 138:1–8	_____	_____
		_____
Psalm 121:1–8	_____	_____
		_____

Preview

It is difficult to know what one's basic motives are. So many
things influence our destinies that most of us find it difficult
to discover one motive behind an action. But often enough
we can see that one motive or value is stronger than the
others. Below are listed various motives. Some of them may
have predominated in various things you did during the last
day or two. If you can think of things you did principally for
the reasons listed below, jot them down.

1. To please God _____

_____

2. To learn more about something _____

_____

3. To help me grow _____

_____

4. To show love or to make myself more lovable _____

_____

5. To escape pain or suffering of any kind _____

_____

6. To enjoy it _____

_____

7. To make my life a little more secure _____

_____

8. Other reasons _____

_____

4

The Call to a New Life

There was a certain Pharisee who invited Jesus to dine with him. Jesus went to the Pharisee's home and reclined to eat. A woman known in the town to be a sinner learned that he was dining in the Pharisee's home. She brought in a vase of perfumed oil and stood behind him at his feet, weeping so that her tears fell upon his feet. Then she wiped them with her hair, kissing them and perfuming them with the oil. When his host, the Pharisee, saw this, he said to himself, "If this man were a prophet, he would know who and what sort of woman this is that touches him—that she is a sinner."

In answer to his thoughts, Jesus said to him, "Simon, I have something to propose to you."

"Teacher," he said, "speak."

"Two men owed money to a certain money-lender, one owed a total of five hundred coins, the other fifty. Since neither was able to repay, he wrote off both debts. Which of them was more grateful to him?" Simon answered, "He, I presume, to whom he remitted the larger sum." Jesus said to him: "You are right."

Turning to the woman, he said to Simon: "You see this woman? I came to your home and you provided me with no water for my feet. She has washed my feet with her tears and wiped them with her hair. You gave me no kiss, but she has not ceased kissing my feet since I entered. You did not anoint my head with oil, but she has anointed my feet with perfume. I tell you, that is why her many sins are forgiven—because

of her great love. Little is forgiven the one whose love
is small."

(Luke 7:44–47)

The woman must have stood far back on the fringe of
the crowd the first time she came upon Jesus. It was curiosity
that drew her that time, no doubt. But as she watched this
man and began to listen to what he was saying her skepticism
must have melted little by little until it came to be replaced
by wonder, admiration, and at length, real affection. This
Jesus spoke of something for which she hungered but had
never known—love. This in itself would not have moved
her. Quite the contrary. How often she had heard this word
bandied about. How often she herself had used it, or rather
misused it. But with Jesus she finally had to admit the word
sounded different. He *meant* what he said. He knew what
love was all about. He loved people. His compassion, his
concern, his tenderness towards everyone, especially the
underdogs, the outcasts—the sinners—proved beyond all
doubt that he meant what he said.

Whether it was all finally ripening into love she didn't
know. All she did know was that now she found that she was
being strongly attracted to Jesus and all that he stood for.
She desperately wanted the kind of love Jesus talked about
and the kind he gave. She could no longer bear the spurious
kind she had been involved in with her casual "loves."

Now she stood in the crowd outside the house where
Jesus was at dinner. She felt dismay and indignation. There
was Jesus with the dust of the road still clinging to his feet.
The host, in his deliberate rudeness, had not offered the
common courtesy of providing the customary foot-washing.
Jesus was hot and tired, unrefreshed, neglected. She could
bear it no longer. Ignoring the protests and taunts, she
pushed her way through the crowd. Ignoring, too, the
shocked expressions on the faces of the host and the guests
reclining at table, she burst into the room, made directly for
Jesus, and threw herself at his feet. Then the torrent of love,
contrition—all the thoughts and feelings that had been fer-
menting within her—burst forth in a flood of tears that lit-

erally bathed the feet of him whom she knew in her heart now she wanted to call "Master."

There is no need to speculate and analyze here. Jesus has done it for us. This woman's love was so great, he explained, that it was enough to wipe out years of self-indulgence, contempt for others, pride, cruelty—all the things that come under the heading of what we call "sin."

The words Jesus spoke to this woman tell us a great deal. "Your faith has saved you. Go in peace." It began with faith, with the woman's response to Jesus as she stood on the fringe of the crowd. At first the response was grudging, conditioned, tentative. It was a response or rather a series of responses first to a message but after a while to a man. Gradually the woman began to accept the truth of what Jesus said. Later she found that it was Jesus himself she was inclined to accept. She found that she was coming to believe in him, to have faith in him. But it wasn't really a matter of a sudden abrupt change of heart. It wasn't a firm decision, made once and never questioned. The woman must have wondered that evening whether this new life Jesus offered was really all that valuable. Would it be wise to turn her back on the old life, the old ways? The next morning things must have looked even more unreal. There might well have been days, weeks, even months of resolutions half-made, re-made, withdrawn, modified. After all, if she did make a decision to follow Jesus, there was the question of how far she should go, of how much of herself she would be willing or able to give. Eventually, the woman did join the band of loyal and devoted women who went about with Jesus and his disciples. They ministered to them and served the people as well. But this complete involvement, too, must have come about by degrees. At first, there were more frequent trips to hear Jesus as he preached. Then, there was a bit of sharing in the things the women and the other disciples did. Finally, there came the gradual acceptance of more and more responsibility, deeper involvement in the life and work of Jesus and his followers.

What this woman experienced and responded to was the call of God to faith and to a change of her way of living.

As it always does, this call demanded the taking of a risk. The woman was asked to give up a way of life which was, in some respects, easy and pleasurable and familiar. But once the woman went ahead and took the risk, she found unexpected pleasure and joy—the companionship and support of the other followers of Jesus and the peace and true love which comes when one's heart is set on God.

Jesus expressed the call to conversion very simply when he said, "Reform your lives and believe in the Gospel" *(Mark 1:15)*. Reform often has negative connotations. People think of it as giving up ways of acting which often are pleasurable and which usually are familiar and comfortable. Actually, *reform* means re-shaping, making one's life new in the way God calls us to do. This way is laid out in the Gospels, in the beatitudes and the sayings of Jesus. Each person hears the call of God again and again in specific, usually ordinary ways, to make over his or her way of acting, thinking, and being.

While this process involves risk and difficulty and even at times failure and discouragement, God promises that new ways of acting will gradually bring greater "love, joy, peace, patient endurance, kindness, generosity, faith, mildness and chastity" *(Galatians 5:22–23)*.

Questions
- **To what kind of life are we called by God?**
- **How am I to know what God wants me to be and to do?**
- **How can I discover whether the direction of my life is in accord with what God is calling me to become?**

What Kind of Life

We are called by God to become more fully members of a people. God is constantly working to bring people together as members of his one family. Therefore, he is always seeking to create and intensify our community with others. The hallmark of that community is to be love and concern for others.

God always calls us to grow in the direction of living our love. He wants us to become better human beings, to become more loving and lovable people. He calls us to grow in sensitivity to the pain of others and in our realization that often it is we who are the cause of pain in others. He calls us to look not only at what we do but also at what we fail to do. Too often we fail to reconcile people, to hold up hope to others, to affirm and encourage others, to help those we can help. God calls us to say "no" to ourselves in certain things in order that we may say "yes" to others, to those who are in need of material things, and more importantly, to those who are in need of our friendship and our love. He calls us from a too self-centered way of life which involves either doing harm, consciously or unconsciously, to others and to the environment, or at least not doing what I might do.

What God Wants Me to Be and Do

Usually, the will of God is made known to me by the circumstances of my life. A few people feel an extraordinary push to do some special task for God. However, most people are called to do their ordinary tasks in life—working, recreating, living in family or alone—in a loving way.

Some people think God has a master plan for each person, worked out to the last detail. They think all we have to do is discover this plan so that we can try to live it out. In reality, God's plan is more simple. God has put our lives into our hands, and all he asks is that we use our unique talents to be loving human beings in the circumstances of our lives in which we find ourselves or in which we put ourselves.

Discovering the Direction
God Wants Me to Take

It is Catholic teaching that the will of God for me is to

develop to my full potential as a human being and a child of God within the family of faith. For a great many people who have always been growing in this direction, discovering the direction God wants their lives to take does not require fundamental changes. It may be merely a matter of intensifying one's efforts. Even in the case of those who feel that they are pursuing wrong goals, it is often a case rather of going about seeking the right goals in the wrong way—a way that will not promote their growth.

To discover the consistent, overall direction my life is really taking, I need to examine not only what I do as a rule but also *why* I do the things I do. I need to look at my ideals, my principles, my goals. Above all, I need to determine what, in actual fact, are my values.

Our lives are guided by many values and beliefs. These values and beliefs are not of equal importance. In fact there are only a few of them that are basic or ultimate values, those which are more important to me than all the others, those which give meaning to my life, those which I feel will give me ultimate satisfaction.

These basic values are not the same for everyone. What motivates one person very strongly may not motivate another person at all or to any great extent.

In each individual case, therefore, a person needs to discover what, in the overall picture and for him or her, are these basic values. For Jesus, the one basic value was the will of his Father. Everything Jesus did, therefore—his preaching, his miracles, his ministry to the people, his acceptance of his crucifixion—all were in line with this basic value. All were motivated by it.

Few indeed have the single-mindedness of Jesus. But everyone is motivated, as he was, by some basic value or values. To discover whether we are moving in the direction God wants us to take, we need to discover what in very fact are the basic values which motivate us and then see how they correspond to God's will for us—our growth in humanity and holiness.

Difficulties

In striving to live out God's call, we are apt to encounter
at least three basic problems.

1. *Lack of clarity.* It is not always clear how the Gospel message applies in a given situation. We may have to
struggle with the questions: "What is God saying to me right
now, in this situation? What changes am I called upon to
deal with here and now?"

2. *Selfishness.* I have the natural urge to put myself
first and desire to control others, to be master of my own
destiny. My will may seem more important than God's will
for me.

3. *Self-deception.* Because of prevailing attitudes and
practices in our culture, I may have become so insensitive
to Gospel values that I deceive myself into thinking that God
is my ultimate value while that ultimate value actually is
greed, pleasure, power, or some other form of self-satisfac-
tion. Self-deception often causes me to do the right thing for
the wrong reason. It causes me to think I am on the right
track when actually I am on the wrong one, moving away
from God rather than towards him.

We usually experience some ambivalence, some indecisiveness, some struggle, and conflict within ourselves when

we try to change our behavior and to move towards what we think God wants us to become. In working through these difficulties we can expect to experience not only success and a feeling of well-being but also failure and periods of discouragement and depression.

Very often, we do not realize what our real values are. We think that those things we *say* are important to us and which we *say* guide our lives really are important and really do guide our lives. In reality, we often do not recognize or admit the principles which do actually guide us. The ambivalence, the indecisiveness, or the conflict we feel often comes from the fact that our professed values are not our real values. In conversion, God calls us to become more honest with ourselves so that we can more easily and more openly decide whether or not we want to accept the call to be and do what he desires us to be and do.

Overcoming These Difficulties

Once I see that certain things in my life need to be changed, I can set about to develop new habits, new ways of acting, which will eventually change the old patterns. For such an endeavor, I need to be patient with myself, to cultivate perseverance, and to rely on my sense of humor.

I need to be open and honest with myself. It is so easy to give, even to ourselves, the "right," the "virtuous," or the "expected" answer. We are quick to conclude, without honest reflection, that the things which motivate me are these "good" and "right" things. It is necessary, therefore, in clarifying my values, to examine not what I *say* but what I *do* (together with motive, goals, etc.). It is necessary, first of all, to isolate these values of mine not in the light of morality (whether they are in themselves moral or immoral, good or bad), but simply as to whether they are or are not active and real in my life. Having determined what my *actual* (not merely stated) values are, I can go about comparing them with the Gospels and see how they stack up with God's will for my growth and development.

The process of discovering our basic values and beliefs is long and slow. But we can begin by asking ourselves a series of questions about any statement which we believe expresses a very important and basic value in our life. We have to question whether we freely chose that position and whether our actions and attitudes are consistent with that position.

1. Have I chosen this value from among alternatives—rather than having accepted it because it was the only thing at hand?

2. Did I consider the consequences of each alternative before choosing the one I chose?

3. Did I choose freely, rather than having this "value" imposed on me by someone or something outside of myself?

4. Have I acted consistently in accord with this "value"—been honest in my dealings as a rule, time after time—rather than just now and then?

5. Have other actions not directly related to this value been affected by this position?

6. Am I proud of what I have chosen? Do I experience peace with my choice? Am I willing to state my position publicly?

It will help me a great deal if I can find another person with whom I can be quite open and honest about myself and my motivations—someone who will be a confidant, a spiritual guide.

God's Help

God speaks to us in more ways than we are apt to realize. He speaks to us in the very ordinary events of everyday life, through other people, even through our mistakes, our faults, and our failures. If we learn to listen and to recognize the voice of God in these things, we can gain great understanding, assurance, and strength.

God gives us assurance of success in spite of the difficulties and failures we experience. This assurance is contained in the simple phrase spoken so often in the Scripture,

"I am with you." This assurance comes time and time again at Mass when the celebrant says, "The Lord be with you." These words are not merely a request for God's help. They are a ringing declaration that God *is* with us and that his presence assures our success in our efforts to enter the kingdom.

THE CHRISTIAN COMMUNITY

Jesus called his followers to a life of holiness, a way of life so exalted that it would serve as a model for others. He said that they were to be "the salt of the earth," "a city seated on a mountain," and set as their ideal—a life of self-sacrificing love like his own, a life of such holiness that it would reflect the very holiness of God, their Father.

The problem which has faced the Church from the beginning is how to help the followers of Jesus live up to this ideal. How does one apply the words and ideals of Jesus to the present situation? How much should be demanded? Is the same required or even expected of everyone? How can we distinguish between true zeal and fanaticism, between hopeless idealism and reasonable, attainable goals?

Various individuals within the Church have sought to solve these problems in their own way. They have adopted a rule of life, a manner of living for themselves and those who chose to join with them. This was the origin of the many and varied religious communities within the Church, recognized and approved by the Church.

But the Church has never been allowed to forget that it is composed of sinners and that it must constantly strive to encourage its members to lives of holiness while not making demands on everyone which are too much to bear.

Throughout the centuries the Church has put forth recommendations about prayer, fasting, self-denial, participation in worship, etc. Many of these practices which were encouraged, even expected as a matter of course, became, in time, matters of obligation. They were taught by moral theologians to be binding under pain of sin. This was the case in such things as the obligation of Sunday Mass, the Lenten fast, and Friday abstinence. The inevitable problem was and is that such things tend to become so institutionalized that they come to be regarded as obligations while people lose sight of their original purpose and intent.

Throughout history the Church has also responded as a community to the call of Jesus to care for others and help alleviate suffering and poverty. Religious communities, dioceses, and parishes have established services for this purpose—schools, hospitals, orphanages, homes for the aging, etc. Once again, the problem here is that of *institutionalization*, when these services become routine and matter of fact—smacking more of business than of charity.

The Church itself has to face the problem of institutionalism within itself. There is always the temptation to withdraw from concern for the world into a sort of corporate ivory tower and think that people exist for the institution rather than that the institution exists for people.

But the Church is people, and the Holy Spirit continues to work within those people. Therefore, new ways of adapting, new ways of ministering, new ways of serving the world, and new ways of continuing in the struggle to grow always come forth within the Christian community.

PERSONAL PROFILE

It is crucial that we know our values and our motivations. It is even more crucial that we understand how these values and motivations operate in our lives. In this section of the Personal Profile, you have an opportunity to analyze a specific action of yours. You have the opportunity, too, to grow in your contact with God—your ability to hear and respond to his call.

Review

Every important action we do reflects, at least implicitly, what is really important to us. It is not always easy to become conscious of our values, but we can try by constantly asking ourselves WHY?

1. Write down an important action you have done recently:

_____

_____

2. Answer these questions.

● What other choices did I have? _____

_____

_____

● What did I hope to get out of what I did? _____

_____

_____

● Why did I decide to do what I did? _____

_____

● What was the basic or fundamental value I saw in what

I did? _____

_____

_____

NOTE: The following is an example of how this exercise works.
● I married Nancy.
● I could have married someone else or remained single.
● Advantage? Companionship, love, security, convenience.
● Why? I loved her.
● Value? I need someone to love me and for me to love.

Prayer

People get in touch with what is really going on within them and express it in different ways. Some people feel most comfortable using words. Others can do best by using images, pictures, or bodily motion. When we pray, we should feel free to use the method which helps us most. Read the following passages and write, draw a picture, or move your hands, arms, or entire body to express how you feel and what you want to say to God. These passages show us that the Word of God frequently calls us to a life of love—a life of letting go.

● *Jeremiah 31:31–34.* The new covenant, the new way of life to which God calls us is of the heart.

● *Ezekiel 36:24–29.* The Lord will give us a new heart and place new life within us.

● *Matthew 5:1–12*. The happiness promised those who re-form, re-new their lives according to the Gospel call.

● *Matthew 6:1–4*. Loving acts are to be done, not for show, but out of love for God and one's neighbor.

● *Matthew 7:24–29*. Anyone who lives the Gospel message of love gains wisdom.

Preview

There are many definitions of sin. Most, if not all of them, contain an insight into the nature of sin and evil. Reflect on how you would describe or explain or define sin and write your answer here:

I think sin is _____

_____

because _____

_____

_____

_____

_____

5 Our Struggle to Respond

It was a joyful reunion. The seventy disciples that Jesus had sent out to announce his coming to the towns and villages around the countryside had come trooping back. They were flushed with the glow of success. In excited tones they exchanged their stories with one another. They surrounded Jesus and, talking at once, each seeking his attention, they reported the joyful news, "Lord, even the demons are subject to us in your name!"

Jesus was pleased. He smiled his approval and encouragement. And yet at the same time he added a note of warning. Things will not always go so well, so smoothly. You will encounter difficulties as you go along day by day striving to respond to my summons—this was the burden of his warning *(Luke 10:17–18)*.

By this time the twelve apostles understood this warning of Jesus a little better. They, too, had felt this first fervor. In the beginning, it had all looked so easy. "Come, follow me," Jesus had said. They had simply set aside their nets and gone off with him—gone off to a new and wonderful and exciting life. And it did indeed prove to be new and wonderful. But at the same time it did not turn out to be the totally blissful experience they had expected.

Troubles arose from the outside, from the apathy and sometimes the hostility of the people, and even from the inside—from themselves. They saw the crowds who had at first responded to Jesus with such enthusiasm turn aside from him and walk away when his message proved to be different from their expectations. They found that others who were not of their group were preaching and working miracles in the name of Jesus, and they were chagrined and—yes, they had to admit it—jealous. They felt the open hostility of the authorities, who watched their every move and showed very plainly that they were scandalized by what they saw and heard.

Worst of all, the disciples found that they themselves were not the completely transformed individuals they thought they would become once they said *yes* to Jesus and made their decision to follow him. They found themselves at times filled with rage and burning with an ignoble desire for vengeance. They went so far as to suggest to Jesus that he call down fire from heaven to consume the people who refused to respond to him. They found themselves arguing and bickering among themselves, jockeying for position, and fighting over who would have a higher place in the kingdom.

The disciples would find, later, that other old weaknesses would surface. Peter would act impetuously and violently, drawing his sword and cutting off a man's ear. Afterwards, he would deny with an oath that he even knew Jesus. And the others, all except John, would run away and hide when Jesus was taken prisoner. Even after Pentecost when the Holy Spirit manifested his presence in the church, we find that Paul and Mark did not get along *(Acts 15:36–39)* and that some converts such as Ananias and Sapphira did not give themselves wholeheartedly to following the way *(Acts 5:1–10)*.

What these highly favored, chosen men were coming to grips with, what Jesus reminded the seventy disciples of and warned them about was the fact of sin. They encountered sin which caused people to close their ears to the message of Christ or even to persecute Jesus and his followers.

For all their close association with Jesus and not withstanding their wholehearted decision to follow him in the new life, these men came into contact with their own sinfulness. They were wounded men. Their woundedness became all the more apparent to them as they strove day by day to respond to the summons of Jesus.

The apostles became aware of their sinfulness, as all people do who honestly confront themselves. But these men dealt with this woundedness of theirs, not by despairing of overcoming it, not by shrugging it off but by coming to Jesus with it. One of them, Judas, did despair. But Peter and the others sought the loving, comforting, and healing power of Jesus. Gradually, day by day as they labored in his cause, they grew in strength and holiness.

Sinfulness—our own and that of others—is a fact of life that we become aware of early in life. How to deal with sinfulness, guilt, and the effects of sin in our own lives and in the lives of others is an important question that faces everyone. But it is especially important for anyone who is at all serious about living the Christian life. An awareness of our woundedness must be the first step. We need to face the fact that we *are* sinners, not only victims of the sins of others but persons who freely and deliberately commit sin ourselves. Seeking and availing ourselves of the means of dealing with our sinfulness, the means offered by Jesus and our fellow members of the Christian community is the next, ever ongoing step.

Questions
- **How do we experience our woundedness?**
- **How can we strive to ovecome our woundedness?**

Woundedness

We experience our woundedness in the pull of that inner tendency which tends to hinder us from living out the call we receive from God to become more loving people, more perfect human beings. Saint Paul gives eloquent testimony to this tendency, "I cannot even understand my own actions. I do not do what I want to do, but what I hate. What happens is that I do, not the good I will to do, but the evil I do not intend. But if I do what is against my will, it is not I who do it, but sin dwells in me" *(Romans 7:15–20)*.

In addition to this *tendency* we find within ourselves there is the matter of our personal sins and the effect they have had on us.

We find that at times we actually *do things to harm others*.

- Stealing, cheating, lying, killing, committing adultery.
- Using people as things rather than treating them as human beings.
- Participating in the unjust practices of our society.

Finally, we discover that we are capable of *turning completely from God,* of ignoring him if we do not outright reject him. We try to live our lives without God as if we alone were masters of our lives.

We find that what others say or do (or fail to say or do), whether malicious or well-intended, may cause us to react in ways that are negative and harmful to our growth. We may acquire a poor self-image, an inability to relate well to others, or a preoccupation with self that causes us to turn inward to an unhealthy extent.

An Optimistic View of Human Nature

The Catholic position on human nature and original sin has always been a basically optimistic and hopeful one. It has consistently opposed the idea that we are so sinful by nature that all God can do is "cover us over with the merits of Christ" and *regard* us as worthwhile and holy if we have accepted Jesus as our Savior. The Catholic teaching has always been that we are wounded by original sin but remain basically good and capable of holiness and growth in holiness with God's help.

We can strive to overcome our woundedness by realizing that we are able to do so with the help of God and by cooperating with Jesus and the means he offers us to deal with our woundedness and overcome it.

Questions
- **What temptations are we apt to encounter as we attempt to deal with our sinfulness and woundedness?**
- **How can we deal with our sinfulness and woundedness?**

Passing the Buck

The first temptation we are apt to encounter is that of trying to shift the blame to someone or something else. This tendency is beautifully brought out in the story of the sin of Adam and Eve *(Genesis 3:1–19)*.

One does not need to take the story literally in order to see the inspired ingenuity with which the sacred author brings out God's message that tells us what sin does. The garden, the tree, the fruit—all these are merely figures to bring out the sacred meaning. The message is in the process. This is what tells us what sin is, what it does, how it affects us and others.

Notice the effect the sin has on the man. He hides from God. He becomes evasive. When he can no longer hide, he seeks to escape responsibility. He puts the blame on another—on the woman and even, in a subtly suggestive way on God. "The woman you gave me," he says, as if, somehow, it is God's fault after all. Then the woman, when confronted, does likewise. "It wasn't my fault, really," she says in effect, "It was the serpent. He deceived me."

We find ourselves acting like the man and woman in the garden story. They couldn't bear to stand naked before God; they had to "cover up" both literally, with fig leaves, and figuratively, with excuses and evasions. We find ourselves doing the same thing. We find it hard to be open and candid with ourselves, with each other, and with God. We conceal our real motives from others, from ourselves, and even, we hope, from God. We *rationalize*, blame others, blame the culture, make excuses, lie, fail to communicate, and find all sorts of ways to hide from others, from God, and even from ourselves.

We are apt to encounter the temptation to justify our selfish and immoderate attitudes and behavior, to rationalize about them, and write them off as negligible or even try to convince ourselves that they are right and good.

We may be inclined to be blind to our faults and simply not acknowledge them.

Finally, we may be tempted to use the "cop-out" of despair, saying to ourselves that, since we cannot overcome our weakness and sinfulness we might as well not try to.

Healing

The first step is to acknowledge that we are sinners, to admit our woundedness and take responsibility for our attitudes and behavior, not making light of our sins, blaming others, shrugging them off as inevitable and excusable because "everybody does it."

After acknowledging our faults, the next step is to try to make amends to those we have injured when it is possible to do so.

After we have looked honestly at ourselves and our weakness, we find hope and strength by looking to God, by prayer, opening ourselves to his forgiving and saving power. It is a great help to realize that God is ever willing to heal us if we come to him honestly as sinners instead of trying to present ourselves to him as innocent and righteous.

We sometimes fail to grow because we nurture old wounds, pitying ourselves, blaming others—people or circumstances—and reacting negatively and even destructively in our relations with others because of something that is over and done, about which we can do nothing anymore.

In dealing with old wounds such as these we need to recognize the stages we go through and consciously work through them.

- The tendency to deny that we have been hurt—simply to refuse to see the problem at all.
- The stage of anger—blaming everyone else and taking bitter consolation in anger and resentment.
- The stage of depression—turning the anger into ourself and blaming ourself for letting others hurt us.
- The stage of acceptance—trying to understand, to forgive, to see how we may have learned from our painful experiences, and to use them as a means of growth rather than of stagnation or retrogression.

A vital point in dealing with our sinfulness and woundedness is that of seeking and accepting help from others. Others can be objective, can see what we might not be able to, and are often willing to give advice and help if they see that we want it.

The Christian community, the Church, has lived with and dealt with the problems of human weakness and sinfulness for centuries. The wisdom and help of the Church is necessary for us in dealing with our own sinfulness and woundedness.

The Church teaches us to judge our responsibility and our guilt according to whether we sinned out of weakness or malice. We need to judge the extent to which we have impaired our relationship with God who loves us and our relationship with our neighbor.

As Jesus himself did, the Church teaches us to make a distinction between the sins we commit because of human weakness and those that we commit out of malice. Jesus was gentle and forgiving with the woman taken in adultery, with Peter in his impetuous act of violence when he cut off a man's ear, and even with Peter in his denial, which stemmed from fear and cowardice rather than malice. He was much more stern with the sins of those who deliberately closed their hearts to the plight of the poor and the oppressed and those who stopped their ears against John the Baptist and against him because they preferred to cling to their positions of wealth and power rather than open themselves to the truth.

Jesus also made a distinction between those who sinned by selfishness but did not close themselves off completely from God their Father and their neighbor—the son who at first refused to do the chores for his father but later relented, the publicans who stole but were aware of their sinfulness and repented—and those who persevered in their selfishness, insensitivity to others, and self-imposed blindness. Among the latter were those Pharisees of whom he said, "You will die in your sins" and the rich man in the parable who was so closed in on himself that he did not even notice Lazarus, the beggar who lay starving at his gate.

The Church teaches that there is a real distinction between *mortal* sins which destroy our relationship to God—those by which we turn away in a complete and serious manner from the love we should have for our neighbor and for God—and venial sins which weaken or harm these relationships without destroying them.

The Church gives us principles and guidelines in these matters. But the Church tells us that it is one's own conscience that must decide what is right or wrong and that it is one's own conscience that is to be followed in judging and acting.

Conscience is the judgment a person makes as to whether or not an action or a refusal to act builds up, tears down or even destroys the relationship he or she has with others and with God. Conscience can easily be swayed or misdirected by the wounded tendencies of our nature. It needs to be enlightened by reason and guided by the teachings of the Church. In the last analysis, however, it decides what is or is not sin for the individual.

Questions
- How do the sins and the woundedness of other people affect us?
- How does the sin of the world affect us?
- As adult Christians, how do we respond to the reality of the sins of others and of the world?
- How is God present to us as we strive to deal with our own sinfulness, that of others, and that of the world?

The Sin of Others

The sin and the woundedness of others affect us in that people who are significant to us, such as parents and teachers, at times model ways of acting and teach things which are contrary to the spirit of the Gospel. Some people hurt us especially in relationships so that we are tempted to close up and refuse to take a risk again of trusting people. Finally, there are people who actually try to hinder us from responding to God's call.

The Sin of the World

The sin of the world, which is embedded in culture and institutions, often makes us blind to the injustice and lack of love which is in the world. We accept things as they are, not realizing how they violate others and the call of the Gospel. In fact, we even accept the rationalization for such injustices that are offered by society.

We see the sin of the world in the lack of harmony among people in living and working together.

There is mutual mistrust, cut-throat competition, dog-eat-dog attitude in business and life—the arms race, created "shortages" for the sake of increased profits, selfish demands of corporations and labor unions, oppressive governments, unjust court systems, the justification and glorification of war, etc.

There is exploitation of people and things. The world is treated all too often not as a gift and a responsibility to be cherished and reverenced but as something to be seized and exploited. People are regarded as something to be manipulated and used for selfish ends, regardless of the effect on them and their lives.

There is a general attitude of not wanting to become "involved," of letting injustice, oppression, and suffering go on rather than going to the bother of attempting to do anything about the situation.

The Reality of Sin

As adult Christians, we respond to the reality of sin in others and in the world by recognizing that we all share in the sinful condition of the human race. All people and all institutions are in need of salvation. We try to have patience, understanding and compassion for others, while striving to remedy injustice and oppression rather than allowing ourselves to become indifferent, cynical, or despairing about conditions.

The well-known *Serenity Prayer* of Alcoholics Anonymous expresses the Christian attitude quite neatly: "God, grant me the serenity to accept the things I cannot change; the courage to change the things I can; and the wisdom to know the difference."

The Christian's awareness of the reality of sin makes for a realistic attitude towards people and the world. It prevents wide-eyed idealism—the kind that believes that people will always act nobly and be unfailingly selfless and good if conditions are right. On the other hand, Murphy's Law ("whatever can go wrong will") does not always have to be taken into consideration. The Christian can have a hopeful and optimistic realism, founded on the conviction that people are still basically good and will respond in some way to faith and love and trust. Christians also share the conviction that God's grace is present and operating in people and in the world. Above all, the Christian's awareness of the reality of sin prompts him or her to accept responsibility for doing whatever he or she can do to make things better and to help other people.

Presence of God

God helps us deal with sin in the most wonderful way of all. Through Jesus he has assured us that we and other people and the world we live in are worthwhile. He assures us that he loves people no matter what they do. His love for them never wavers even when they turn from him. Because we can never know all that is involved in our actions, God assures us that we will be judged on how well we tried rather on how well we did.

Moreover, God is able to speak to us and reveal himself to us even through our sins. Sin is fatal only when we do not learn from it. From our sins and failings and from the sins and failings of others we can learn that God loves us even though we are weak. We need to change and we need God's help. If we recognize this, then sin can actually turn out to be helpful for our growth.

Finally, through the Spirit whom he sends to us, God strengthens us so that we can continually strive to tame the tendencies to sin that are within us. God does not magically remove us from the sinful environment in which we live or kill the tendencies to sin that remain within us. But he does provide the strength we need to take whatever steps we must take to weaken the power sin can exercise over us. God also holds out constant, inexhaustible forgiveness and renewed hope, no matter how often or how seriously we fail.

THE CHRISTIAN COMMUNITY

The Christian community, made up as it is of individuals who are imperfect and wounded, is itself imperfect and wounded. The community itself can be guilty of injustice, arrogance, pride, greed, worldliness, ambition—in short, of all the vices which can sometimes appear in its individual members. The community needs to take its measure and judge itself continually in the light of the Gospels.

It is the constant temptation of the Church to become guilty of institutionalism—the attitude that the institution exists in its own right, to be served by the people, to dominate, to use power as a weapon, to wrap itself in the mantle of religion and become itself an idol. For this reason the Church must always remind itself that it is *people,* that its organization exists to serve the People of God rather than to be served by them.

Christians today have no difficulty in accepting the fact that the People of God in the Old Testament, even though they were God's chosen people especially dear to him, remained a sinful people in constant need of God's help. God had to send them prophet after prophet to console them, to castigate them, warn them, and remind them of their identity and their mission. Time and again the people deviated from their purpose and became worldly, arrogant, guilty of injustice, and unfaithful to the covenant. Today, we are not upset by this fact. We realize that even a people specially favored by God remain human, imperfect, and in constant need of help from God to bring them back to their destiny.

Some Christians do not have the same understanding attitude towards the People of God in the New Testament. Often enough, the reason why some look for utter perfection and undeviating holiness in the Christian Church is that they themselves are affected by *triumphalism*—the notion that we are a sinless and perfect people and that the Church should be infallible in the sense that it can never be guilty of infidelity to itself, to others, and to God and that it is never in need of God's corrective efforts.

Individuals in the Church sometimes suffer from the faults, weakness, sins, and excesses which the community can exhibit. It is not to condone such faults, sins, and excesses to say that, rather than merely condemning them or opting out of the Church in disgust, the individual members are called upon to show compassion and understanding. Members can call upon their sense of humor, their knowledge of history, and their understanding of the Gospel to help them work to remedy a bad situation.

Saint Paul compared the Church to the human body. The comparison is very apt. If the Son of God in taking a human nature did not exempt that nature from the limitations to which human nature itself is subject, neither did he exempt his Church from the limitations inherent in any organism whose members are sinful human beings.

The Church will be perfect at the end of time when God's Kingdom will be fully realized and manifest. Meanwhile, it is the task of all the members to work patiently to help build it up and purify it day by day.

PERSONAL PROFILE

Our struggle to find ourselves and to belong to a community can go unnoticed. It is a good idea to record from time to time some of our reflections and prayers concerning the fact of struggle and our own woundedness.

Review

Sacred Scripture continually calls our attention to the fact that God always takes the initiative and reaches out to his weak, helpless, and sinful people. Reflect on the following episodes, in which Jesus reached out to people in need of help. Think of those things in your life which make you feel weak, helpless, or sinful in a way similar to the people in the story. Speak to God about how you feel. If you wish, jot down how you see yourself similar to the people in the story.

I see in myself

● *Mark 1:32–39*   Jesus confronts the evil of the demons and disease which oppressed the people.   _____

● *Mark 6:45–51*   Jesus calms the fear and panic of the disciples.   _____

● *Mark 9:14–29*   Jesus comes to the aid of a possessed boy.   _____

● *Mark 10:35–45*   The patience of Jesus with the disciples who did not understand his message of selfless service for others.   _____

● *Mark 14:66–72*   Peter, though he is an apostle, denies Jesus.   _____

Prayer

We all experience the effects of wounded human nature in our lives. Centuries ago the Psalmist had the same experience. In his pain he cried out to God for help. Read some of the things said in *Psalm 38* and then compose your own cry of anguish, asking God's help and telling him of the sin and woundedness you experience.

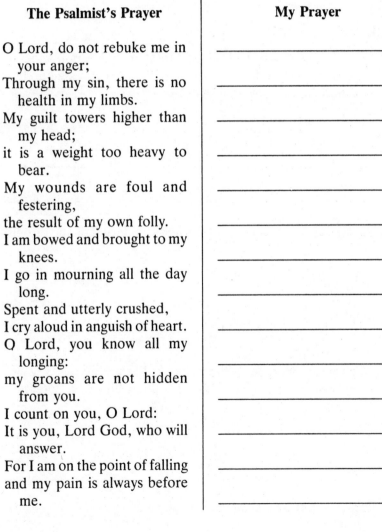

The Psalmist's Prayer	My Prayer
O Lord, do not rebuke me in your anger; Through my sin, there is no health in my limbs. My guilt towers higher than my head; it is a weight too heavy to bear. My wounds are foul and festering, the result of my own folly. I am bowed and brought to my knees. I go in mourning all the day long. Spent and utterly crushed, I cry aloud in anguish of heart. O Lord, you know all my longing: my groans are not hidden from you. I count on you, O Lord: It is you, Lord God, who will answer. For I am on the point of falling and my pain is always before me.	

I confess that I am guilty
and my sins fill me with dismay.
O Lord, do not forsake me!
My God, do not stay afar off!
Make haste and come to my
  help,
O Lord, my God, my savior!
(Psalm 38)

Preview

Read the story of the call of Moses in chapters 3 and 4 of
the Book of Exodus. List the fears Moses expressed and the
excuses he used to avoid God's call.

_____

_____

_____

How did God answer Moses's fears, and what did he promise

Moses? _____

_____

_____

Can you remember a time in your life when you were sure
God was calling you and you offered all sorts of fears as
excuses for not following the call?

_____

_____

How did God answer your fears? _____

6

God Heals and Strengthens Us

When Pharaoh let the Israelites go, God led them by way of the desert road toward the Red Sea. The Lord preceded them, in the daytime by means of a column of cloud to show them the way, and at night by means of a column of fire to give them light. Neither the column of cloud by day nor the column of fire by night ever left its place in front of the people.

(Exodus 13:17–22)

In these words the writer of the book of Exodus is telling us that God, who called Moses to lead his people out of Egypt, was present and active in the lives of those people at all times. The Bible goes on to describe God's presence and activity in book after book of the Old Testament. Moses, the leader, is always intensely aware of that presence. He communes with God in prayer. He brings God's message to the people and is forever reassuring them. He constantly reminds them that God loves them, that he is deeply involved with them in their sufferings and trials, and that he will always be there to fulfill his promises and help bring their hopes to fruition.

Even after the death of Moses God's presence and activity continued. The leaders of the people and those who were reflective and prayerful were aware of that presence even in the ordinary stuff of their lives. The people tended to become worldly, to rely on their own strength, to envy the material prosperity of the pagans around them, and to imitate their behavior, adopt their mores, and even share their beliefs. Far from abandoning the people when they drifted away or even rebelled against him, God was always the more eager to rescue them. Often enough it took a calamity to make people aware once again of their need for God. When faced with a famine or an invasion by hostile neighbors, the people would express their renewed awareness of the need for God. They would cry out to him for help. And, invariably, God, who had been present among them all along, would respond and come to their aid.

In general, we are more aware of God's presence in the world today and we have a better understanding of his activity. We learn from our catechism to say that God is everywhere—not off somewhere remote in the sky. We understand, in speaking of God's providence, that he cares for all of us and actively strives to help us to holiness and salvation. Those who cultivate a sense of God's presence and seek closer intimacy with God through prayer can actually arrive at the stage wherein they are so well aware of God's loving presence that they may be said to live in the presence of God. This is the blessing which comes in the process of conversion when one has responded and cooperated day by day with God's grace. It is the blessing which comes as one's life is becoming transformed. It is a force which aids a person's ongoing transformation.

The intimate, loving presence of God is what is known as the state of grace. God is present everywhere. He is present not only in creation but also within the hearts and souls of people. It is God's intent that his presence within us be a presence which can warm us as fire in a furnace warms and transforms a piece of iron. And God's presence does have this effect in the souls of those who do not frustrate God's efforts by an obstacle such as serious sin. God's warming, life-giving presence has its effect on those who are trying to live up to their call. This intimate, loving presence is so real that it is described as "sharing God's life." When it is realized, reciprocated and fostered, it becomes a source of deep inner joy and peace and a powerful incentive to serve others and to grow in love of God and neighbor.

Those who live in the state of loving awareness of God's presence in their lives find that slowly and gradually their lives are transformed. They begin to see things in a different light. What was once thought to be very important comes to be regarded as unimportant, and things once viewed as unimportant or not considered at all become primary values. Self-centeredness gives way to concern for others and the problems and pain they face. There grows a desire to become involved in the struggle to work for the good of other people.

Even in the midst of trials and sufferings, there comes a deep and abiding inner peace. This is the blessing Jesus promised to those who respond to his summons and strive day by day to live in the presence of God. "My peace is my gift to you. I do not give it to you as the world gives peace. You will grieve for a time, but your grief will be turned to joy. Your hearts will rejoice with a joy no one can take from you" *(John 14:27, 16:20, 22).*

Questions

● **How does the blessing of God's presence in our life become a reality for us?**

● **How can we respond, once we have recognized God's presence in our life?**

● **What problems are apt to arise which may make it more difficult for us to affirm God's presence in our life?**

● **What help do we have to deal with these problems?**

He Is Present

Too often, we think of God as being off in outer space somewhere, aware of us but nonetheless outside of us. In reality, God is dynamically present within me. The first step in causing God's presence to become a reality for me is to realize that God does permeate my very being and is constantly seeking to elicit from me a loving response to his interior presence. To make such a response I need to recognize my sinfulness, my weakness, and my need for God. With this realization, when I turn humbly and confidently to God dwelling within me, that divine presence becomes a meaningful reality for me and I become open to God's strength, encouragement, support and, above all, God's love.

Surrender

We can respond to the recognition of God's presence by surrendering ourselves completely to the loving care and power of God. This surrender means that one no longer needs to figure out everything for himself or herself, and that one can begin to put oneself in the hands of God:

- *With prayerful gratitude,* which expresses itself not only in communal or liturgical prayer but also in personal, private prayer in which one listens to God and speaks to him intimately.
- *With trust,* which is the deep conviction of God's love for me, and that even this present pain or trial will prove to have been a blessing and that God's presence will enable one to deal well with the situation.
- *With generosity,* which is a willingness to share one's faith and confidence in God's presence with others and to give others support and comfort in their trials.

Problems

One of the greatest problems is that material things are too close to us. It sometimes seems to us that things we can see, feel, and touch are the only realities. Things of the spirit are apt to seem not only remote but also unreal.

Added to this problem are the problems which arise from our own basic self-doubt. Seeing ourselves with all our sins and weaknesses, we may be inclined to think that we are so unworthy that God could not be concerned about us or could not seek a union of love with us. In this state of mind we may be prey to two tendencies:

- The denial that God is truly present within me, seeking my response, to dismiss whatever indications I may have as tricks of my imagination.
- Despair—to think either that God wouldn't bother with me or that the problems are too great to be overcome.

Then, too, the problem of passivity may arise. I may be inclined to take God for granted, assume that God will take care of everything without any need of responsibility on my part.

Helps

God is constantly awaiting our response to his invitations. The means we have for such a response is prayer. Prayer can take a number of forms. Basically, it is attention to God, being in God's presence, listening, and communicating with God. Prayer may be prompted not only by a desire to become closer to God in love but sometimes by pain, by desperation, even by anger. We call upon God in whatever our want or need, realizing that we are sinful and unworthy. Nevertheless, God is present and ready to respond. For meaningful prayer certain conditions are necessary:

- *Silence.* We need to put aside many distractions that beset us in our ordinary daily routine and to assume an attitude of listening to God instead of doing all the talking ourselves.
- *Reflection.* We come to some better understanding when we think back over our life, when we analyze what has

happened and is happening. We need to be open to how God is constantly seeking our growth and ultimate happiness even in our trials and sufferings.

Questions
- What are some of the problems we meet in prayer?
- Is there a "best" way to pray?
- How can we integrate our prayer with the Word of God in Scripture?
- How does Jesus help us as we try to pray?

Problems

Some see prayer *only* as formulas—ready-made prayers which others have composed. Others think of prayer not only as set forms of words but as long, tedious and often flowery and stilted formulas. Some have the notion that prayer is simply a duty, something hard and onerous that one *ought* to engage in, something that belongs only to certain hours and certain occasions.

Some have the idea that there are various methods of praying and these are the only options one has when one wishes to pray. There is also the idea that certain "higher" forms of prayer are only for a few chosen souls and are beyond the reach of ordinary people.

If we think of prayer as a "listening presence" we begin to see that the problem has its origin not in our prayer itself but in our general habits and behavior, which we carry with us into our prayer.

If we are in the habit of jumping from the past to the future in our thoughts instead of focusing our attention on the present moment, we will naturally adopt this same procedure when we try to pray. In this way, we will actually be courting distractions.

Perhaps, when we are with others, we don't give them our full attention. Maybe we don't really listen to what they are saying but are busy thinking of what we are going to say when they pause for breath. If this is the case, we have not disciplined ourselves to be fully *present* to others. It follows, then, that we will not be fully present to God when we attempt to pray. If we are the kind of person who does all the talking, we will do all the talking when we pray instead of first listening to God and then responding in our own way.

Questions
- **Is there a best way of praying for everyone or are there different ways for different people?**
- **What are some various ways to pray?**

Ways to Pray

Since each person is unique, with his or her special temperament and experience, each person's way of praying is to some extent, unique to that person. The ideas and suggestions of others are valuable and even necessary as general guides and helps. But they should be just that and not hard and fast systems to which everyone should conform. Extroverts will find prayer that is concerned with others and with outside events more natural for them. Introverts will be more attracted to and more at home with looking inward in their prayers. People who need regular routines will need familiar formulas and set rituals in prayer. Other people will respond better to impromptu situations and will be happier with freer, more spontaneous types of prayer.

There are certain basics which everyone needs—some silence and reflection, for example. But each individual can find from among the many methods and kinds of prayer which the Church has to offer, certain ones which fit that individual, and then, adapt whatever he or she wants to use to individual needs and preferences.

Everyone engages in a continual dialogue within his or her own mind. Comments, questions, and statements are part of the inner dialogue of our conscious life. This continual conversation with self is part of our consciousness. Frequent prayer can change this dialogue. Through this inner dialogue with God people can become more aware of the God-within them.

Prayer and Scripture

One can pray the prayers which are to be found in the Scriptures—the Magnificat *(Luke 1:46–55)*, the Benedictus *(Luke 1:68–79)*, the Psalms, the prayer of Judith *(Judith 9:2–14)*. One can put oneself as it were "in the shoes of" people or objects in the Scriptures and let oneself experience and react as they might have, and then respond to God in prayer.

One can enter into imaginative dialogue with Jesus as one who reads what he said or did, asking why, making comments, etc. One can read a passage of Scripture slowly and thoughtfully and then close one's eyes, reflect on what has been read and then, with or without words, express to God what one thinks or experiences.

Jesus Helps Us Pray

Jesus helps us by his example. As we read in the Gospels how Jesus prayed, we discover how we, too, can communicate with God and live in his presence *(John 17, Mark 14:35–36, John 11:41, 42)*.

The vision of Jesus is alive and active. True to his promise, he is with us whenever we gather with others to pray *(Matthew 18:20)*. But he is also within us by means of the Holy Spirit, prompting us, encouraging us, inspiring us. If we strive to be aware of his presence within us, we can come to pray more and more as he did.

THE CHRISTIAN COMMUNITY

The Church is a People, a people reaching out beyond themselves, seeking God, seeking wholeness, and seeking salvation and the fullness of life. One of the strong bonds which holds these people together is this common goal and the common experience of contact with Jesus Christ. And that experience is kept alive, nourished, and relived day after day, year after year, century after century by what is called *ritual*. Ritual is a symbolic act or event which has a deeper meaning than is evident in the very act or event itself. The simple act of eating is an example. We eat because we are hungry or because we need food to sustain us. This is all that is evident on the face of it. But when we eat together in celebration of a wedding, a birthday, or some other social event, we do so in order to exhibit and enhance unity and community. In this case the act of eating becomes a ritual. Like all rituals, such a communal meal puts us in touch with a reality that would not be made visible in any other way.

Rituals are essential, then, in the life of the Church. The primary rituals of the Church are those which comprise its liturgy.

The Church's liturgy is the official prayer of the People of God. As such, it differs from private or individual prayer. Since liturgy is official prayer, it must express the experience not of an individual or a group of individuals, but that of the entire community. It must, therefore, be more general, more universal, more formal and stylized than popular devotions, which can serve more individual tastes and more specialized needs.

This is not to say that the official liturgy (mainly, the Eucharistic Celebration) need be a cold, rigid ritual in which one cannot find personal involvement. Nor is it to say that the Mass and the celebration of the sacraments must always take the same form with rites and language and formulas which never change. Quite the contrary, these rituals, so essential to the life of the Church, need to be kept meaningful and moving.

Church ritual, like everything else in the Church, must be constantly subject to reform and renewal. The Eucharist was originally celebrated in Aramaic and was essentially in the form of a meal. Languages and forms changed again and again throughout the centuries. Because for four hundred years, in reaction to the Protestant Reformation, there was little or no change, some took it for granted that changes in these matters were never normal or necessary.

One problem which confronts parishes today is that of making the official liturgy something living, meaningful, and appealing. People cannot expect to have a deep spiritual experience every time they take part in the Mass. We always have to deal with the ups and downs that go with temperament and life situations. But the Church officially insists on good celebration and urges care and devotion in its rituals. The Church invites us to open ourselves up to the liturgy and to enter into its spirit.

In short, members of the community have the right to expect and to seek the good and meaningful celebrations of the liturgy.

PERSONAL PROFILE

The strength and healing of God is felt in moments of prayer. But it is a good idea to record personal attitudes and experiences of prayer. Use this opportunity to take an inventory of how you experience prayer.

Review

Reflect upon a time when you have felt God's presence in your life most strongly. Describe the circumstances, what

you felt, what you did, what the effect of the encounter was
in your life.

_____

_____

_____

_____

     At times it helps us to reflect on the condition of our
prayer life.

- When I pray I feel that I am really present to God about
  ___% of the time.

- When I pray I feel that God is really present to me about
  ___% of the time.

- I spend about ___% of my prayer time in listening
  to God.

- As I go about my daily activities I am listening about
  ___% of the time for what God is saying to me through
  them.

- About ___% of my prayers are prayers of petition, asking prayers.

- About ___% of my prayers are informal prayers, those
  in which I speak to God in my own words.

The biggest difficulties I find in praying are _____

_____

The greatest consolation I find from praying is _____

_____

_____

Prayer

The great Christian prayer, the Our Father *(Matthew 5:9–13)* is often ignored in private, personal prayer. Each phrase can speak to us, comfort, and confront us. Each phrase can also strengthen our desire to be more aware of our God within us. Take the time to be present to and reflect upon *one* phrase of the prayer. At another time, select another phrase for your prayer.

- Our Father in heaven,

- hallowed be your name,

- your kingdom come,

- your will be done on earth as it is in heaven.

- Give us today our daily bread,

- And forgive us the wrong we have done as we forgive those who wrong us.

- Subject us not to the trial but deliver us from the evil one.

Prayer and spiritual reading can feed and complement each other. Your local bookstore and/or library may contain writings on Christian prayer. Some books which may help you understand your *own* prayer are:

- Edward J. Farrell, *Prayer Is a Hunger, The Father Is Very Fond of Me.*

- Matthew Fox, *On Becoming a Musical Mystical Bear.*

- Thomas Merton, *Life and Holiness, Seeds of Contemplation, Contemplation in a World of Action.*

- Karl Rahner, *Encounters with Silence.*

- Adrian Van Kaam, *Spirituality and the Gentle Life.*

Preview

If I had one wish in each of the following areas of my life, this is what I would like to see happen:

In my relationship to my family (or community) I would like

to see _____

_____

In my relationship to God I would like to see _____

_____

In my relationship to the world in which I live I would like

to see _____

_____

In myself I would like to see _____

_____

In the circumstances of my life I would like to see _____

_____

7

A New Zest for Life

Balancing the empty water pitcher on her head, the woman made her way, as she did every day, to the well which was situated just outside the town. Today was a day like all others—lonely and empty. For company she had only the man she was living with at present. There were no relatives, no children, no friends. The solid citizens of the town shunned her, referring to her as "that woman." And so, she had long ago hardened herself against these people. If they despised her, she would despise them in return. If they passed her on the street without speaking, she would ignore them, too.

As the woman drew near to the well, she noted, with a stab of uneasiness, that a man was sitting beside it. He was a stranger and, of all things, a Jew—here in Samaria, hostile territory. She felt within her the feeling of defensiveness and aversion that all Samaritans felt in the presence of a Jew, and she steeled herself to ignore this man, simply to pretend he wasn't there. She would refrain from even looking at him. She would fill her pitcher and go on about her business.

To the woman's astonishment the man spoke to her as she approached the well. He spoke, he smiled, and, wonder of wonders, he was actually asking a favor. "Would she be so kind as to give him a drink of water?"

All the woman could do was voice her astonishment, "How is it that you, a Jew, would speak to me, a Samaritan and a woman, and ask for a drink of water?" she asked. Instead of answering her question directly, the man came out with something mysterious and endlessly intriguing. "If you knew the gift of God and who it is that is speaking to you, you would, perhaps, ask him and he would give you living water."

The gift of God, living water! Who was this man and what on earth was he offering her? Forgetting her antagonism, unease, and embarrassment, the woman laid down her pitcher and gave this stranger her full attention. She asked question after question. "What about this so-called sacred well? What about the Jewish-Samaritan question? Where was the proper place to go to worship God?"

The stranger answered her questions patiently and politely. And then, Jesus (for the stranger was Jesus) gently began to speak about the woman's life, her multiple marriages, her relationship with the man she had recently taken up with. But Jesus was not condemning. He was calling her to a change of her life, but in a caring, hopeful, non-threatening, and positive way.

By now, the woman had ceased to ask questions, much less make excuses. She listened, she opened her heart and soul as well as her ears to what this prophet was saying to her.

Then, all too soon, this unbelievable encounter was at an end. The apostles were returning from their shopping in town, filled with wonder at the time and attention Jesus was giving to this Samaritan woman.

She scrambled to her feet, hastily dusted herself off and, forgetting her water pitcher, ran back into town. And this notoriously unfriendly, defiant woman found herself stopping people on the street, telling them in excited, breathless tones about this Jesus she had discovered and urging them to go out and see for themselves.

The woman, whose name we don't even know, drops from history at this point. The Gospels tell us nothing further about her. But there can be no doubt that her life from that day on was different. It could not have been a magical trans-formation, a metamorphosis that progressed without set-backs, without periods of doubt, anguish, and suffering. The old habits would not die overnight. The old temptations would recur again and again. But, all this notwithstanding, the woman's life was changed. There was a new purpose, a new direction, and if her life was not a smooth and un-troubled advance, we can presume that it was, on the whole, a steady one. The woman had responded to the summons of Jesus—the summons to a new life. And the result was that gradually her life underwent a transformation. We can picture her looking back over the months and years as time went by, and finding that things which she had once thought she could never get along without were not really important to her after all. Conversely, she discovered that other things of which she had never been aware had become values in her life. Previously, her life had been self-centered. Now, she realized, she was more concerned about the welfare of other people. The woman became aware, too, that gradually, as time went on, her attitude and her disposition had changed. Now she was more optimistic, more cheerful. Her life had a purpose. She had found a zest for living that she had never known in the old days.

Her view of herself had undergone a change, too. No longer was there that deep down self-loathing which ex-pressed itself in an "I don't care" attitude about herself and her life. Now there was a conviction of self-worth that im-pelled her to undertake tasks she would have thought herself incapable of doing. She acquired a confident belief that she could grow and become a better person—a more useful, more productive member of the community of which she now was definitely a part.

The transformation of life which we assume occurred in the case of this Samaritan woman is the transformation of life which takes place in the life of anyone who undergoes a true process of conversion. After a person has responded to God's call, has sought God's help in dealing with the woundedness and weakness that is a result of sin, and has become aware of the presence of God, a new sensitivity comes into his or her life. Gradually, there comes about a transformation which expresses itself in a new way of looking at life and a new way of living. This is the state of being and way of living of which Jesus spoke when he said that in order to belong to his kingdom a person must be "born again" *(John 3:1-8)*.

This process of regeneration and rebirth goes on again and again. One who has recognized and reacted to God's dynamic presence within is now open to and docile to succeeding calls from God and becomes aware of ever new areas of life—areas which were heretofore closed to God's activity. Such a person responds again and again, meets and struggles with more difficulties and in so doing finds still greater zest for living and still deeper meaning in life.

It should not be assumed, however, that this process is automatic or irreversible. A person can lose heart, retrogress, turn away, and finally revert to the way of thinking and living which marked him or her before this conversion. And even when one is progressing and growing as a result of the conversion process there can be setbacks, temporary failures, or discouragements along with the successes and observable progress. But, as long as the fundamental process is still going on, even with the apparent setbacks, as long as the effort to grow and live a new life continues, growth is taking place and the new life is becoming ever more sturdy and vigorous.

Questions
- **How do we come to know that our life is being transformed in the process of conversion?**
- **How do we respond when we come to this realization?**

Life Transformed

We come to know that our life is becoming transformed when we become aware that our general attitude is becoming more and more one of enthusiasm rather than boredom. We are becoming more interested in people and things rather than diffident about them. We are becoming more open to others, more trusting, more willing to reach out. Instead of a "put down" attitude about ourselves and our abilities, there is a growing sense of self-esteem. Instead of a feeling of alienation and isolation, there is a sense of belonging and an interest in the life and work of the community.

Overall, there comes into being the state which Saint Paul describes when he enumerates the qualities that mark a person who truly lives in the spirit of prayer and the presence of God. These are the qualities which are sometimes referred to as the "fruits of the Spirit: love, joy, peace, patient endurance, kindness, generosity, faith, mildness, and chastity" *(Galatians 5:22, 23)*.

The Response

We respond by making prayer a more important factor in daily life, by sharing the new zest for life and love with others, by reaching out to and affirming others, by joining with other like-minded people, and by working with others to help alleviate pain and suffering and to eliminate injustice.

Saint Paul provides a good example of how one who is truly undergoing conversion responds to God's grace. Paul's first response to God's call, after seeking out the man God sent him to for help, was to go into seclusion and pray. Afterwards, he went down to Jerusalem and aligned himself with the apostles and the Christian community. He found new strength and resources within himself. He used his energies now in a positive way—in apostolic work for the Kingdom of Christ. He broke his connection with old companions and associations which might have pulled him back to his old ways. He worked with zest and enthusiasm in the cause of bringing the knowledge of Christ to others.

Questions
- What problems are we apt to encounter in our efforts to live a new life?
- How does a mature Christian face these problems?

Problems

In the process of conversion and personal transformation there are several problems that we can encounter. These problems are real and can have a very great impact on us.

1. The problem of *comfort*. It is hard to change and adopt new ways of being and doing. It is much easier and more comfortable to go on 'exactly as before. Change and effort can be painful. Pain is something everyone wishes to avoid if possible.

2. The problem of *ridicule* or the fear of ridicule.

3. The problem of *doubt*. When we become discouraged, doubtful about the reality of God's presence and his love for us, the prospect of risk and change becomes all the more unattractive. In the process of conversion second thoughts, doubts, and misgivings can easily arise. It is then much easier to give up and return to the more familiar ways of thinking and doing.

How Mature Christians Respond

Mature Christians realize that problems are to be expected. They recall that Jesus and his followers faced strong opposition and many problems during their lives. They understand that God does not call us to a trouble-free and comfortable life. He does call us to a life of love.

Mature Christians realize that they need to strengthen their conviction that God's presence and love are real and that his promise to be with us is a promise that we will succeed in our efforts. They are aware that prayer is an absolute necessity.

They seek the support and encouragement of other people who share their faith, convictions and efforts to live the new way of life.

Mature Christians strive to maintain their conviction that they can really overcome the sin and woundedness they experience in their own nature, and that they can be effective in working against the evil they see at work in the world in which they live.

A person who is trying to live in a new way may be strongly tempted to think, "What can I do to make even a small dent in such problems as racial strife, poverty, injustice, war, etc.?"

The first thing we can all do is become conscious that there are many real problems existing on our doorstep. The values and practices of the society in which we live are not always in accord with Christian ideals and principles. The mature Christian weighs popular ideas and opinions and even the laws and directives of the government in the light of the Gospels. He or she does not take as a guide to attitude or behavior the maxim, "Everybody thinks this way nowadays," or "The government says that this is what I must do. It must be okay."

Secondly, a person trying to live a Gospel-oriented life realizes that the problems are huge, and that there are so many of them that one will become burnt out and frustrated if he or she tries to become involved in too many causes. A person responding to God's call need not try to become involved in all the good causes that exist, but he or she does need to become involved in at least one effort to combat the sins of the world and to join forces with others who are working in that field. The old saying expresses the mature Christian attitude when it says that it is better to light one little candle than to curse the darkness.

THE CHRISTIAN COMMUNITY

The conversion process which brings about the state marked by a new zest for life has been called *re-birth*. It is principally a re-birth into a community of faith. Jesus himself spoke about it this way. In his conversation with Nicodemus, the learned Pharisee who came to him by night, Jesus said that anyone who would become a member of his kingdom must be born again. Quite understandably, Nicodemus was puzzled by these words. "How can a man be born again once he is old?" he asked. "Can he return to his mother's womb and be born over again?" Jesus explained that the re-birth he was referring to was a spiritual not a physical one, begetting of "water and Spirit" *(John 3:1–5)*.

The re-birth, then, comes about through Baptism. But mere submission to the ritual of Baptism would not accomplish the conversion of life of which we have been speaking here. The new way of being and doing comes about when we have responded to God's calls and have come to live day by day in a community which responds to his continued calls. Saint Paul was at pains to point out to his converts that now as baptized Christians they were called to live in a new way, with new values, new ideals, new insights, and consequently a new, more positive, more productive, more creative, more God and neighbor-centered way of life.

Paul writes to his converts of Ephesus:

> I declare and solemnly attest in the Lord that you must no longer live as the pagans do—their minds empty, their understanding darkened. They are estranged from a life in God because of their ignorance and their resistance; without remorse they have abandoned themselves to lust and the indulgence of every sort of lewd conduct. That is not what you learned when you learned Christ! I am supposing, of course, that he has preached and taught to you in accord with the truth that is in Jesus: namely, that you must lay aside your former way of life and the old self which deteriorates through illusion and desire, and acquire a fresh, spiritual way of think-

ing. You must put on that new man created in God's image, whose justice and holiness are both of truth.

(Ephesians 4:17–24)

The converts to whom Paul was writing had been pagans. Hence the reference to a former way of life which is described as darkness. But Paul makes it clear in his total message that conversion is not by any means always a process of change from a state of absolute darkness or gross sinfulness to a Christian way of life. His own life is a case in point. Paul was a good Jew—a firm believer, faithful to the law of Moses and the worship of the true God. Yet he professes again and again that he was reborn himself and his whole life and viewpoint changed and was transformed when he became converted to Christ. And the message of the Gospels is the same—conversion need not involve a change from total darkness and sinfulness to a new way of being and doing. It can also be a change from a good life to a better, more intense, more positive, more creative and fulfilling life in the family of faith.

PERSONAL PROFILE

The conversion experience is a call to a "new lease on life." So often, we forget the moment of conversion. So, it is a good idea to take time to recall the experience and to record the feelings which may have accompanied the experience. Use this opportunity to do just that. This is an opportunity to spend some time in serious reflection on the nature of the conversion experience.

Review

Think of one situation in your life in which you think you had a conversion experience—in something very large or in something not so large. There was a call, a response, encountering difficulties, prayer, and a new way of being.

In what way did the call come?

_____

_____

What was your life like in this particular area before the call?

_____

_____

_____

How did you express your response?

_____

_____

_____

What difficulties did you experience in trying to answer the call?

_____

_____

_____

Was there any prayer; if so, what was it like?

_____

_____

_____

_____

_____

What did you do to overcome the difficulties you experienced?

_____

_____

_____

_____

What is your life like in this regard, now that you feel that you have entered into new life?

_____

_____

_____

_____

_____

Prayer

Conversion is an experience which awakens and deepens one's conviction about one's coming *from* God, about one's returning *to* God, and especially that one is *of* God—one is a child of God, loved and cared for by God. Select one of the Scripture passages below which describes and speaks to you about *your* present conviction.

● *Micah 6:8.* Do the right, love goodness and walk humbly with your God.

● *Jeremiah 24:7.* I will give them a heart. They shall be my people and I will be their God, coming back to me with all their hearts.

● *Psalm 51.* Have mercy on me, O God. A clean heart create for me, O God, and a steadfast spirit renew within me.

● *Psalm 85.* You have restored the well-being of Jacob.

● *Psalm 91.* Say to the Lord, my refuge and my fortress, my God in whom I trust.

● *Hosea 6:1–3.* Come, let us return to the Lord. He will heal us; he will bind our wounds. He will come to us like the rain, like spring rain that waters the earth.

● *Hosea 11.* The early love of God's children, then, their infidelity, and again God's call to conversion. God speaks in these words to me. "How can I give you up? My heart is overwhelmed, my pity is stirred. I will not let the flames consume you."

Preview

The next section of this book is concerned with our turning to Christ. Below are a series of questions to test your knowledge about him. Mark the answer *True* or *False* or *Don't Know.*

_____ Jesus was as human as we are.

_____ Jesus, today, is no longer a man.

_____ Jesus is alive today.

_____ Jesus knew all things from his childhood on.

_____ Jesus had to learn just as we have to learn.

_____ Jesus still has human consciousness and human feelings.

_____ Jesus had sexuality.

_____ Jesus liked some people more than others.

_____ Jesus looked and acted like a man but he was really God.

_____ Jesus did not have feelings of anger, despair, affection, desire, etc.

_____ Jesus grew as a person through his relationships with his family and friends.

_____ The life of Jesus in the New Testament is historical biography.

_____ Jesus hims.!f made the decision to die for us on the cross.

_____ Jesus lived his life according to a plan worked out by God from all eternity.

_____ Jesus spent a great deal of time teaching religious doctrine.

_____ Jesus kept all the Jewish laws and regulations.

_____ Jesus can serve as a realistic model for my life.

8

Jesus Shows Us How to Lead The New Life

We sit at the table, about to begin a meal. We reach for a fork—not a spoon, not a knife, but a fork, because we realize that this is the right utensil. We reply to a question. We don't utter primitive cries or resort to charade-like gestures. It is words, the right words, that spring to our lips. We wonder what time it is. With the utmost ease we glance at the watch we wear on our wrist. We know what the numbers mean and what they indicate.

Few of us can recall when it was or how it came about that we learned to eat properly, to speak intelligently, to tell time, to do all the things which are part of everyday living. But one thing is certain: It was some person or persons who taught us. And that person or persons usually taught us not by mere words but by embodying in themselves the things we learned about life and living. It happened this way in all the phases and aspects of life. Our parents, our teachers, someone, or various people who showed us how to live and how to act.

But the need we had for such models did not vanish when we emerged from childhood. Even in adult life, when we stand at a crossroads, when we are confronted with some new challenge, we often feel the need not for written directions but for a person who not only tells us but also shows us how to be and how to act. We may well find ourselves in such a situation at the present time. We have been concerned about the calls to conversion—the invitations to further growth that God is giving us. We have been considering the direction in which God is seeking to guide us. We have come face to face with our weaknesses, our sinfulness, and the state of sinfulness we find in the world about us. We may have gained some insight into the changes that might be made, the tasks that could be performed. But all this could have served to put us at a crossroads. Where do we go? How do we begin? What direction can we take? How are we to proceed, given our weaknesses and the problems that lie ahead? These may well be questions that trouble us in our efforts to respond to God's call. At times like this we especially need a model to show us the way.

These same questions troubled the earliest Christians, too. They were aware that, by Baptism, they had responded to a call from God to a higher, more perfect way of life. This was a call which had come to them through Jesus, who said, "Be perfect as your heavenly Father is perfect."

But for day-by-day living these early followers of Jesus were very much aware that they needed guide-lines, directives that would enable them to live this higher life day by day. And rules and regulations would not be enough. They had these in the Mosaic Law. What they needed now, they saw, was a living model, a person who embodied the kind of life they felt they were called to. And, of course, it was Jesus himself who embodied this life. And had he not said, "Learn of me" and "no one comes to the Father except through me"?

As question after question arose, these early Christians would seek out those who had walked and talked with Jesus. The believers wanted to listen to those who had heard from Jesus' own lips the message he had given and had observed how he himself lived and acted day by day. This is how the New Testament came to be written. People would ask, "What did Jesus say about how to use material possessions? How did he act in this matter?" And the apostles in their letters and the evangelists in their gospels addressed themselves to such questions as they put into writing their memories of what Jesus said and did.

But these Christians did not merely look to a Jesus who had lived and died, they also realized that Jesus was risen. He was alive and was with them helping them to respond in their own way to this call. Paul, for example, realized that the risen Christ wanted him to preach the Gospel to the Gentiles, that the risen Christ was with him when he faced persecution and when his own weariness held him back. Paul and most of the early Christians never knew Jesus before his crucifixion, but they did know him as risen Lord. They did know that through his Spirit he was guiding and helping them.

As the Church grew and spread, its members came gradually to gain deeper insights into the message of Jesus and into Jesus himself, not merely as the carpenter of Galilee but as the Lord—alive, present, and active in their lives. They came to know him better by discerning the Spirit of Jesus at work in the Church. They learned of him in prayerful reflection on the written Scripture and by their participation in the life of the Christian community. They also came to know him better in the breaking of bread.

In modern times the situation is vastly more complex, but the basic issue is the same. For Christians today, as in the earliest times, it is the living Jesus himself—Jesus who is the way, the truth and the life—who embodies the life which his followers believe they are called to live. Christians today look to the Spirit of the risen Jesus for help and guidance as well as to Jesus as they find him in Scripture and in the Church. It is the living Jesus who not only tells us but actually *shows* us how to respond to God's call, how to deal with evil and sin, how to live, and how to die.

Questions
● How do we learn from Jesus how we can respond to God's call to life?
● What does it mean to me to "live as Jesus lived"?
● What does the life of Jesus tell me about my life?

Learn From Jesus

The call of God is a call to believe in the living Jesus—to live and to die as he did. From Jesus we learn how to respond in trust and faith to God's call as we struggle with our weakness and with sin in our efforts to live out the mission God has given us. In him we see the new life that is born in those who believe. As we look to Jesus as our model, we do not see a blueprint of what we are to do. Rather, we see the underlying attitudes which guided Jesus in the face of evil to live out the mission God gave him and which led him through death to achieve a new life.

We come to know Jesus as one who is his own unique self. Jesus refused to fit himself into the roles into which others tried to place him. Jesus was *his own man*. He believed in and lived according to the values and principles he espoused and preached, no matter how strong the pull to turn aside from them—the approval of the authorities, the expectations of the people, the offer of a crown, and worldly success.

Jesus was, above all, a *man for others*. He had more than kind words for the poor, the oppressed, and those who were discriminated against and looked down upon. He positively *identified* with these people, went out to them. He felt for them and *with* them. He *consoled* people in their suffering, not as an outsider but as one who understood and related to them fully. He was patient with the weakness, inconsistency, and lack of understanding he found in others. Jesus strove at all times to raise people up, to manifest love and concern, and to *give strength* to the weak and *courage* to those who needed assurance and affirmation.

Jesus, My Model

Endeavoring to live as Jesus lived does not, of course, mean trying to do the things he did or imitating his life-style. Rather, it is a question of making our own the values and principles he lived by. It means seeking to have the *attitude*

Jesus had about God, himself, other people, and life itself.

- **About God.** Jesus manifested the deepest love for his Father—a constant endeavor to do God's will. His trust in the Father was complete. He was utterly convinced that what the Father wanted for him was what was best for him, for his growth, his welfare, and his ultimate happiness.
- **About himself.** Jesus was his own man. He did not try to pattern himself on others. He knew that God wanted him to develop and grow as his unique self. He knew and achieved his own true identity. He accepted and cherished who he was.
- **About others.** Jesus saw every person as unique, as an individual, as a person with whom he identified as a human being, and as a brother or sister. He did not stand apart from others and deal out favors in the manner of a philanthropist. He gave of *himself.* He gave unstintingly—not to a few, but to everyone who asked his favor. He so identified himself with others that he was extremely sensitive to their needs. This was especially true of the poor, the distressed, and the suffering ones—those who were passed over and neglected by others.
- **About life.** Jesus saw life as a joyful, positive gift from God. He had a deep reverence for the world and all creation. Far from rejecting the good things of the world, he blessed them and rejoiced in them. At the same time, he relished and constantly preached detachment—not becoming enslaved to anything and thereby losing freedom.

Endeavoring to live as Jesus lived means seeking to have these attitudes towards God, oneself, one's neighbor, and life itself. It means seeking, as Jesus did, to achieve and to accept one's true and unique identity. It means cultivating a deeper sensitivity to the wants and needs of others—an empathy towards others, especially the poor and suffering. It involves an endeavor to grow in strength and to develop one's gifts in order to be of greater service to others and a source of strength and consolation to them. It means that we try to "cross over" and strive to become a *part* of the life and the distress of others, especially of the powerless, the weak, the poor, and the sinner. It means to go to others with one's own failures and weaknesses and short-comings, not fearing humiliation, failure, and disappointments. It means not seeking an ego-trip but rather, a loving identification with others and with their lives.

The life of Jesus shows in the organic pattern of life itself. It puts life and death in perspective by showing us life as a joyful adventure, death as a necessary passage to a greater life, and the risen life of glory as the ultimate goal.

The pattern of life, death, and resurrection occurs again and again in the life of Jesus. Physical death and resurrection were preceded and prepared for by countless "little deaths"— giving up his own preferences when the will of the Father or the welfare of others required it. The inner peace and joy that came as a result made the renunciation worthwhile and life-producing.

And yet, Jesus was guided by faith in these little deaths, and especially when it came down to accepting crucifixion itself. He did not know how it felt to die. He did not have any previous experience of crucifixion. So completely human was he, Son of God though he was, that his day-by-day experience and his acceptance of death was basically the same as ours. The difference was that Jesus had such great trust in God that he entered into life and death at every level with wholehearted acceptance. He trusted that God would give him the ultimate glorious life he hoped for. As he went through this cycle again and again, and especially as he entered into it at the end, he pointed out to us that this is to be the pattern of our life as well.

Questions
- **Does accepting Jesus as my model give me immunity from suffering?**
- **Who is the authentic Jesus I am to accept as a model?**

> ● What are the difficulties I may encounter in trying to have Jesus as a model and how can I overcome them?

Suffering

It would be a return to the land of fairy stories if we were to think that simply accepting Jesus as one's model would insure one's immunity to trouble, pain, and suffering ever afterwards. The life of Jesus himself was by no means free from mental and physical suffering. Jesus never gave a promise that the lives of his followers would be any different. What he does promise is peace of mind, peace of soul, freedom from the dominance of our inordinate desires and appetites—that peace which, he says "the world cannot give." But even this inner peace cannot be expected to come instantaneously and magically. What Jesus promises is help to strive day by day against the forces within us that hold us back and grace to withstand things on the outside which threaten us. Those who have in very fact taken Jesus as their model come to know the inner security of having their own true identity. This is not at all the same thing as that kind of smug and arrogant presumption which says to others, "I am one of the 'saved.' I am *in* and nothing can dislodge me from my safe and secure position." This was precisely the attitude of some of the Pharisees whom Jesus castigated. Accepting Jesus as one's model in the right sense entails humility, charity, concern for others, and a realistic outlook towards life.

The Authentic Vision of Jesus

To have Jesus as one's own model requires that my vision of Jesus be really authentic. There are so many versions of Jesus, so many highly subjective interpretations of him and his message, that a discerning person might well wonder which is reliable, or even whether any of them can be trusted.

After all, what do we know of the historical Jesus apart from the Gospels? When it comes to the Gospels, even the Jesus of faith we find there can be edited in various ways by anyone who undertakes to do so.

All the arguments really point out that we need the living Christian community in order to gain some knowledge of the authentic Jesus. This doesn't mean that every popular devotion, every description of Jesus we may hear in a sermon, every pious book or tract we read is able to give us this knowledge. Some of these can be just as subjective and one-sided as the individual. For real authenticity we must look to the *overall* view that the Church *officially* has and has always had. We see this view reflected in the authentic teaching of the Church. And we see it, most effectively, in the liturgy itself—the prayers we find in the Eucharistic Celebration rather than in private devotions.

Difficulties

It would be an easy matter just to "hit the sawdust trail," claim to have Jesus as one's model and mentor and presume that life from there on would be simple and serene. But whenever we try to answer God's call, the first enthusiasm wears off and we begin to encounter our own weakness, which holds us back, side-tracks us, and may even cause us to give up.

1. I may find it difficult to recognize that particular events are an invitation to growth and even more difficult to recognize and accept the possibility that I can change.

2. My innate scepticism and cynicism may tend to prevent me from taking Jesus seriously as anything more than a shadowy good figure who somehow impinges on my life rather than as one who is alive and a part of my life.

3. My sense of logic may fight against my taking many of the sayings of Jesus to heart. For example, the Beatitudes seem to contradict common sense. This admonition that we become as little children seems to make no sense when we strive all our life to grow up.

4. I may lack confidence in myself to be able to live up to the high ideals presented by Jesus. Past failures and my inconsistency may tempt me to decide that following Jesus is simply beyond my powers. In such a case, I exhibit a lack of confidence not only in myself but also in God and in Jesus.

5. After a time I may be tempted to give up because I had the false expectation that once I accepted Jesus and the call of God all would be well in my life. I find that I am still myself with all my weaknesses and sins—that I still have to struggle.

6. I may find that the price I have to pay is high. I may be required to give up habits and attractions which I like and enjoy but which are contrary to the call and mission God is holding out to me.

7. I may also experience the loneliness that comes from the fact that others do not share my convictions. They scorn both me and my convictions or they see me as hopelessly idealistic.

8. Finally, I may find in myself an attitude that regards Jesus as a figure so remote in history that his life has little or no relevance for me in these complex modern times. I may forget that Jesus is alive and through his Spirit is helping and guiding us in these complex modern times. I may fail to realize that Jesus expects me to make decisions based on the same attitudes he had rather than on an uncritical application of his words to modern life.

THE CHRISTIAN COMMUNITY

The Spirit of Jesus is always with me offering me strength and encouragement most often through the people who come into my life. I, for my part, need to take the risk of faith, of trusting completely that God does care for me and will never let me down.

It is said so often that prayer is necessary that the very expression can turn people off. Nevertheless, in the face of difficulties such as these it is essential that I have support, and prayer is an indispensible means of becoming assured that I have the support of God.

I need especially the quiet type of prayer by which I take a little time each day to withdraw from my daily activities and go deep into myself, as it were to stand quietly and nakedly before God, opening myself to his love. I do not need words as much as quiet and recollection to experience God's presence and help.

If I read the Gospels thoughtfully and prayerfully, I will take courage from the way Jesus met these same problems and the assurance he gives me that I will receive the same strength he received.

But, being human, I will also need the support of others—the support of a community. To bolster my lack of confidence in myself and to withstand the nonsupport or ridicule of others I will need the encouragement of others who are in earnest about growing spiritually and following Jesus more closely. The important thing to keep in mind, however, is that I look for people who are sincerely interested in others and striving humbly (and without losing their sense of humor) to grow spiritually. Mere enthusiastic types are more apt to "turn me off" than encourage me. But those whose spiritual life is really deep and authentic and whose lives are, thereby, lives of service and concern for others will be a source of real support and encouragement.

Finally, the experiences of others can be an encouragement for me. Would Saint Paul have been content to return to his old ways, or would the other apostles? Saint Augustine, who regretted that he gave himself wholeheartedly so late, never tired of saying, "Late have I loved thee, beauty ever ancient ever new."

PERSONAL PROFILE

Coming to know and love Jesus is part of the growth of a Christian. But when it comes to knowing him as a model, it is necessary at times to pause and see just how Jesus is affecting the way you *act*. Use this opportunity to reflect on your own response to Jesus as a model.

Review

Jesus is a model for anyone who wishes to grow to full potential. Jesus, who is a man in the fullest sense, shows us how to be fully human. Compare and contrast your responses to the following items with Jesus' response to God and to others.

● *Jesus trusted his Father.* How do I trust my Father?

_____

_____

● *Jesus reached out to and helped others.* How do I reach out to and help others?

_____

_____

● *Jesus forgave the wrongs others did him.* How do I forgive others for the wrongs they do me?

_____

_____

- *Jesus often spent time apart from the crowds in prayer.* How do I manage my time so as to be free to pray regularly?

_____

_____

Each of us needs to know and to answer the question Jesus posed to his disciples, "Who do *you* say that I am?" In your own words, write *your* answer to the question.

_____

_____

_____

_____

_____

_____

_____

Prayer

Jesus of Nazareth preached with strong conviction. He spoke with authority. He knew who he was before God and was free to speak his truth before others. His listeners were struck by his authority and his conviction. He had the courage of his convictions. Be present to and reflect upon Jesus, the man of convictions.

- *Mark 1:14–20.* The call of the first disciples

- *Mark 1:23–28.* Jesus cures a demoniac

● *Mark 2:1–12.* The awe and amazement of the people who observe Jesus

Jesus teaches and shows his disciples how they are to serve others in humility and charity. Think about and reflect upon the scene in *John 13:1–17,* the washing of the disciples' feet.

● I am Jesus. Am I willing to serve others?

● I am Peter. Am I willing to accept the service and care of another? Am I willing to be open and to accept the love and care of God?

In Saint John's Gospel, Jesus is described to us under many signs and symbols. We can learn in prayer the meaning of Jesus for us by pondering these self-revealing statements of Jesus. Select several of these statements to pray with and reflect upon.

● *John 6:30–58.* I am the bread of life.

● *John 8:12–20.* I am the light of the world.

● *John 10:1–10.* I am the gate.

● *John 10:11–21.* I am the good shepherd.

● *John 11:25–27.* I am the resurrection and the life.

● *John 13:12–17.* I am teacher and Lord.

● *John 14:1–7.* I am the way, and the truth, and the life.

Preview

The human problem of suffering is universally expressed by all people at all times in all eras and in all places. No one is exempt from suffering, pain, loneliness, and distress. Suffering is part of each person's life. What do you think about suffering? How do you respond to the suffering in your life and in the lives of others?

The list below gives some common *felt* responses. Check the boxes which show how you feel about suffering.

Suffering	Yes	No	Perhaps
God is punishing me			
I'm doing something wrong			
People hate me			
Others are wrong			
I avoid it			
I am like Jesus			
No one understands			
I am all alone			
I am used by others			
I am O.K.			
I am so helpless			
God walks with me			

Jesus the Source of Life

The fairy tales in which we took such delight as children always ended with the words "and they lived happily ever after." Our delight came from the fact that because of one magical moment all troubles, all problems, all difficulties were forever swept away.

But these were indeed only fairy tales. In real life it doesn't happen this way. When we are rescued from a bad situation we do not find that we are thereby free for life—immune from now on from trouble, strife, frustration, and suffering. We still need help, encouragement, enlightenment, and strength to meet each new situation—each new problem and difficulty which inevitably will confront us.

We would be trying to live in a fairy-tale land if we believed that when we accept Jesus as Savior all our problems are over, that we will have no more suffering or trials. Salvation is a long and difficult process, as we can see when we look at the lives of apostles.

The apostles were ordinary people. Some were fishermen, one a tax collector, but none were rich or powerful. They accepted the call to follow Jesus and walked with him in Galilee. They felt the exhilaration of being in the company of Jesus and of being in on something new as they traveled from town to town. They basked in the security they felt at having a leader who was confident and courageous—one who could calm their fears, answer their questions, and inspire them with high ideals and a noble cause.

Then their world collapsed. Jesus was taken prisoner and crucified. They were plunged into the depths of despair. They lost faith and had no hope. When the risen Jesus approached them, they did not recognize him. They were sure that they were seeing and hearing things. They could not believe and accept the fact that he was alive. Jesus brought them to the realization that he indeed did live by eating with them, by allowing them to touch him, and by explaining the Scriptures to them. When they accepted the fact that he was alive, Jesus gave them the mission to share this tremendous news with others.

But the apostles did not see how they, weak and confused as they were, could carry out the mission entrusted to them by Jesus. Their weakness and incompetence were too great, the problems too many, the obstacles insurmountable. Jesus knew how they felt and gave his Spirit to them. They experienced this saving power of Jesus in many ways. If they were weak, he was strong. If they were fearful, he was courageous. If they were uncertain and wavering, he was confident and sure.

They knew now that Jesus was indeed their Savior, the one who would share with them his courage, his confidence, and his strength in order to help them work through their own weakness and fear. They lived the new life they had with courage, joy, and conviction in spite of the trials and difficulties they encountered.

They realized that their lives had new meaning and purpose. They perceived themselves and others in a *new* way. They had new and more profound convictions about themselves and others. These simple men and women became joyful, loving, and compassionate rather than judgmental and condemning. They became hopeful rather than apathetic or despairing. No longer did they rely on political and economic power to give them a sense of worth and of mission. Their conviction and commitment to the reality of the risen Christ was the source of their courage. They were grateful for the change. They rejoiced in the richness and newness Jesus had brought into their lives. Finally, they were unwilling to hoard this gift. They were eager to share it, just as Jesus had shared his life with them.

The Acts of the Apostles and the letters of Saint Paul give us a strong clear picture of what salvation meant in the life of one man. Paul of Tarsus was a good God-fearing man who sought to please God by keeping the law as perfectly as he could. At first he saw his mission from God as that of hounding Christians from house to house and from city to city to force them to renounce Jesus. He did not recognize the presence of *Christ* in and among the Christians.

Then came the dramatic incident on the road to Damascus when Paul realized that Jesus was alive. With this recognition came the realization that he had to share this knowledge with others. He had to help them experience the love of God and the power and strength of Jesus as he did.

In his efforts to live out his call, to live as one who had been saved by Christ, Paul felt discouragement, weakness, and failure. He experienced betrayal by friends, misunderstandings with those he loved, and hatred and persecution by enemies. But while experiencing success or failure, joy or sorrow, hunger or plenty, freedom or imprisonment, he was absolutely sure that Christ was with him. The presence of Jesus Christ was strengthening Paul in his weakness, consoling him in his loneliness and loving him in all he did. Paul's response to this love, which he fully realized was undeserved, was to work as hard as he could to strengthen those who were weak, to console those who were lonely and discouraged, to help those in need, in short, to preach Jesus Christ by deed as well as word. Yet at the same time he longed with all his heart to finish the race so he could experience the fullness of the new life which had begun on the road to Damascus.

Questions

● How do I know that I am really availing myself of the salvation Jesus offers?

● What difficulties might I encounter in my efforts to accept Jesus as my Savior?

● What helps do I have to overcome these difficulties?

The Realization of Salvation

I become aware that I am availing myself of this salvation when I realize that I am not content to go on doing nothing about my faults, defects, and negative qualities. I become more aware of the needs of others—more concerned about what I might be able to do to reach out and do more than praying for others or talking about their plight. I become uncomfortable about my complacency, my lack of sensitivity for others, my ivory tower sort of religion, or my lukewarm spiritual life. I find in myself an increasing awareness that Jesus is risen and alive and that he is truly aware of me and loves me. This awareness prompts me to want to share my conviction with others, not only by words or pious phrases but by actual concrete involvement with others.

I find that the fact that God loves me is becoming a reality in my life and not just words which I have heard and repeated. I realize that my sins are forgiven and that I am accepted by him with all my weakness and faults.

I find that I am beginning to challenge the status quo. I begin to ask the hard questions. Why can't all the poor be housed and fed? Why can't natural resources be conserved? Why does corruption need to be a part of the political picture? Why do religious institutions have to be as they are? And I begin to seek answers for these questions, answers which reflect a spirit of love and care for all people, not just for the rich and powerful.

Difficulties and Helps

Salvation does not come easily. Many factors within me make it difficult for me to appreciate the gift Jesus offers me.

1. I may be a *practical atheist*. I can't accept the idea that God is interested in my life, cares for me, or loves me. I may believe in a vague way in a blind, impersonal world-force but not really believe that someone greater than this world cares for me. The good news of the Gospel that the God "whom the heavens cannot contain" cares for me seems to be too good to be true. But the *deepest longings of my heart* tell me it is true if only I believe and accept it.

2. The *cynic* in me says that it is foolhardy to reach out to others because they will not appreciate my efforts and will do me in. The *logician* in me says that the resurrection is an illusion and makes no sense. But the *child* in me, who is open to life—joyful, excited, willing to try something new—helps me discount the cynic and the logician.

3. I would like *a magical or instantaneous transformation* of my life and an easy and quick solution to my problems. But an understanding of the *process of conversion* helps me realize that instant transformations seldom last and sound solutions to problems take time.

4. I am *afraid of challenging* the status quo and of identifying with the underdog. But Jesus says there is *no other way to salvation.* "None of those who cry out, 'Lord, Lord,' will enter the kingdom of God but only the one who does the will of my Father in heaven" *(Matthew 7:21).*

THE CHRISTIAN COMMUNITY

In *Matthew 25:31–46,* Jesus describes the person who is saved as one who feeds the hungry, clothes the naked, houses the homeless, cares for the sick, and visits the imprisoned. In other words, the person who has accepted salvation cares for those in need.

The same criterion exists for the community of salvation—the Church. The Christian community does not manifest salvation by calling on the name of the Lord in words alone. The community has a responsibility to be a community of love and care. The family of faith celebrates the good deeds of Jesus by providing an atmosphere in which all its members can grow in love and concern.

The sign of Jesus' saving actions in the community is the action believers take to change the world. The community of faith welcomes sinners. It does not seek to cause rancor. The community passionately fights injustice, hate, and fear. It does not turn aside and ignore the problems of the world.

In summary, the Christian community lives in its everyday functions and actions the invitation of Jesus, "Come to me, all you who are weary and find life burdensome, and I will refresh you" *(Matthew 11:28).*

PERSONAL PROFILE

The life and teachings of Jesus are a source of growth for those who believe. The teachings of Jesus, however, have to enter into the stuff of everyday life—into the feelings and experiences of believers. Use this opportunity to reflect on how the teachings of Jesus get through to you.

Review

Jesus is the norm and measure of how Christian we are or are not. He shares with us today his courage, his conviction, and his commitment. Within the past six months how often have you referred to the life and teaching of Jesus in the situations of your life. The following chart will help you in your reviewing situations in which the teaching of Jesus had an impact.

Situations	Never	Sometimes	Always
In your loneliness			
In your frustrations			
In your anger			
In financial problems			
In marital problems			
In situations where you wronged others			
In self-indulgence			
In resentments			
In confusion			
In fear and anxiety			
In fatigue			
In grief and sorrow			
In failure			
In success			

Prayer

We are Christian disciples to the degree that we accept and respond to suffering as Jesus did. We enter into and participate in the courage and strength of Jesus when we bear difficulties as Jesus bore his sufferings. In these sufferings Jesus trusted his Father's love and concern for him and relied on his Father's protection and deliverance from the evil which threatened to overcome him. Jesus teaches us to trust our Father as a rock, a shield, a fortress, and a refuge. Select several of these Scripture passages to think about and reflect on.

● *Psalm 3.* But you, O Lord, are my shield.

● *Psalm 7.* O Lord, my God, in you I take refuge.

● *Psalm 16.* O Lord, my portion and my cup.

● *Psalm 18.* O Lord, my rock, my fortress, my deliverer.

In the Gospel of Luke Jesus sets forth the conditions for discipleship. Suffering is part of Christian discipleship. Ponder and pray on *Luke 9:23–27*—take up your cross daily and follow me.

Saint Paul experienced both the joy and pain of Christian discipleship. He exhorts us to be faithful to our call to be disciples of Jesus, children of our Father. Choose one of these passages from Saint Paul. Ponder over it, pray with it, and take it to heart.

● *Romans 12:9–21.* Our love must be sincere.

● *2 Corinthians 4:16–18.* We do not lose heart.

● *Galatians 4:1–7.* We are sons and daughters who cry "Abba," Father.

● *Philippians 2:1–11.* We imitate the humility of Jesus.

Preview

We learn from and are influenced by others in our past who have touched our lives. Sometimes our encounters with these *teachers* were brief; yet they had an impact on our lives. They showed us *how to* do something. They taught us how to handle a difficult situation. They led us to discover how to arrive at an answer or achieve a goal.

List important "how to" people in your life. Indicate what you learned or achieved.

"How To" Person	Skill and/or Wisdom Learned

10 Jesus Calls Us to Personal Growth

The shelves of bookstores are crowded with books on how-to-do things. How to cook Chinese, Italian, or French food; how to repair cars; how to overcome stress. A dozen times a day we ask, "How do I do this?"

The most basic how-to question we ask is "How do I live a productive, fulfilling, and happy life?" We get answers to that question when we turn on the television or look at a newspaper. Investment companies offer us financial security. Deodorants and mouthwashes promise us romance. Psychologists tell us how to become popular. But when we hear and respond to the call of God we discover that there is another and different answer. It is the answer Jesus gave— to love our neighbor as ourselves and to love God with our whole heart, mind, and soul.

When Jesus preached, his listeners naturally asked him questions, the same kind of questions we ask today. One day a member of the ruling class, a man who was rich and powerful, asked Jesus the basic how-to question, "Good teacher, what must I do to share everlasting life?" When Jesus told him to keep the commandments, he replied that he had always kept them. Then Jesus told him to sell what he had, give it to the poor and follow him *(cf. Luke 18:18–23)*.

Another time Jesus told the people that he had not come to destroy or abolish the law. In fact, he said that anyone who broke the least of the prescriptions of the law would be the least in the kingdom of heaven *(cf. Matthew 5:17–19).*

Jesus answered many questions simply by referring to what was written in the law. He said, "You have heard the commandment imposed on your forefathers, 'You shall not commit murder; every murderer shall be liable to judgment.'" He did not tell the people that they could disregard this law. In fact, he extended it by saying that anyone who grows angry with another, abuses another, or holds another in contempt deserves punishment *(cf. Matthew 5:21–22).*

But at other times, Jesus emphasized the principle of love rather than the precepts of the law. He approved the way a lawyer answered his own question (which was the same as that of the rich man from the ruling class) by saying, "You shall love the Lord your God with all your heart, with all your soul, with all your strength and with all your mind; and your neighbor as yourself" *(Luke 10:27).*

Thus we see that Jesus answered how-to questions about life by appealing to law and to love. Yet he rebuked the Pharisees for sticking to the letter of the law and to man-made interpretations of the law when these actually worked against the purpose of the law which was to help people love God, neighbor, and self.

One Sabbath, as Jesus and his disciples were walking through the fields, some of them plucked grain and ate it. The Pharisees objected that these men were breaking the law. Jesus answered that "the sabbath was made for man, not man for the sabbath" *(Mark 2:27).*

Jesus was setting limits on law and saying that its mere observance was not the complete and perfect way to serve God.

Jesus pointed out the tension between law and love. The early Christians struggled with this tension. We know that some wanted Christians to keep the law as perfectly as the good Pharisees did. Others felt that they were completely free from all law and that anything went in the name of love. Peter, John, Paul, Jude, and James all wrote letters to various churches telling them how to live. Various churches and individuals collected sayings of Jesus and stories about him that would help them know better how to live as his followers. These sayings and stories were collected and arranged in the Gospels, which have as their purpose to tell people who Jesus was and what he said. The Gospels were to help the followers of Jesus answer the basic question, "How am I to live?"

All through history the Church has struggled with the question of law and love. Today, we too have to work out this relationship in our own times and in our own lives.

We read in Saint John, "God is love. If God has loved us so, we must have the same love for one another" *(1 John 4:8, 11)*.

Jesus calls us to strive to become perfect "as our heavenly Father is perfect" *(Matthew 5:48)*. We are told that love is the way we become humane and fully human. But the problem is that love is a word so overworked that all too often, it floats on the top of our minds when we hear it. We need to ask ourselves, therefore, "What does it mean to be a truly loving person?"

Saint Paul gives us a marvelous description in his First Letter to the Corinthians, chapter 13. We see love in the concrete, love in action, as we look at the life and person of Jesus.

But the how-to question immediately pops to mind. We can't walk the hills of the Holy Land, feed people, or cure them. Often we do not find specific answers to many of our questions in the Scripture.

We still ask, "How do I treat someone who hurt me or betrayed me?" And the answer is still the same, "Forgive seventy times seven." There are no clear answers in Scripture to our modern questions about nuclear power, multi-national corporations, medical research on cloning, or genetic transformations. On the other hand, we are no longer interested in whether or not we can eat meat sacrificed to idols or whether we must first become Jews before becoming Christians.

We cannot look to Scripture for the answers to all our how-to questions, because the circumstances of our lives are very different from the circumstances of the lives of those who wrote the Scriptures. We realize that in our lives and in society we need law to have order, but at the same time we experience conflict when love indicates a course of action contrary to law. We know that people wiser than ourselves and institutions with long histories of experience have codified ways of acting which promote our growth as truly humane people; yet we find that regulations and laws often stifle the real growth of individuals and society. The how-to-live questions can be satisfactorily answered only by grasping the basic intent and importance of law along with a clear understanding of what the love demonstrated by Jesus and commanded by him really means.

Questions
- **What must I do to become the best kind of person I can become?**
- **What does it mean to become more humane?**
- **What guidelines do I have for becoming more humane?**

The Best Kind of Person

The call we each receive from God in the circumstances of our lives is to follow Jesus and become the best kind of person we can become. This call does not mean that we do the exact things Jesus did. Rather, it means that we develop along the same lines he did. It means that each of us becomes more humane in our own way. We are individuals, one of a kind. The combination of our unique physical characteristics, our unique psychological characteristics, as well as our unique memories, experiences, and environment give each of us different challenges and opportunities for growth. We will, therefore, each become more humane in our own way.

The question then is, "What does it mean to become more humane?" Books have been written on that subject, but the prophet Micah summed it up as well as anyone when he called upon the people "to *do* right, to *love* goodness, and to *walk humbly* with your God" *(Micah 6:8)*.

We have the perfect example of one who did right, loved goodness, and walked humbly with God—Jesus Christ. The guideline he gave his followers was love for God, neighbor, and self. One whose guideline is love is a person whose behavior is guided by genuine concern for others. Such a person helps others to strive to reach their potential, while always leaving them the freedom to be themselves. Such a person trusts in the love and care of God, in the goodness of himself or herself, and in the goodness of others. And even though that trust in others is at times misplaced and the trust in oneself shaken by one's own failures and weaknesses, such a person does not become disillusioned and cynical.

A humane person is open to the love of God and the love of others. Such a person is sensitive to the needs of others, even when those needs are not expressed in words. And, as far as himself/herself is concerned, such a person has the courage to let go of whatever enslaves him or her.

Questions
- Does accepting the guideline Jesus gave mean that law is no longer important in my life?
- What are the advantages of law for me?
- What are the dangers of law?

The Law

The call to life, to become more humane, and more loving is not a call to do the impossible, to change instantaneously into a loving person, or to rid ourselves of all our inhumanity and selfish tendencies in one stroke. It is a call to gradual growth, a call to seek more and more for our guidance in our own convictions molded by love. It is a call gradually to make our own the principles of love and justice which underlie all of God's laws and which should underlie human law.

Advantages of Law

We all need law at the earlier stages of our development. It is essential for infants and children to be told what to do—to brush their teeth or not to take other children's toys. The Israelites needed the Law of Sinai because at that time they were a people who were in the early stages of moral development.

As we grow up and become adults, specific laws are not as necessary. We can move on to principles. "Be kind, take care of your health, etc."

But at any stage of our development we may need the law to help guide us when our internal guidance system is absent, not working, or weak. When we cannot accept the differences and weaknesses of others as deserving our respect, our understanding, our empathy, and sympathy, we need law to protect us from trampling on those people. Law makes us accountable for our actions and keeps our behavior in line with the basic tenets of love, especially for those whom others see as not having rights or as being unworthy of our own care and consideration.

Law is like a dancing teacher who teaches us the basic steps and rules of dance and then sets us free to express in our own way the beauty of the dance, whatever it may be. It guides us as we learn, grow, and mature.

Law remains at all times necessary to delineate the bounds of what we may do and still preserve a minimum of justice. At times we will experience a different mix of law and love, of fear and trust. At one time or in one area we will be more governed by law than by love. At another time or in other areas we will be more governed by love. Very few people's lives are governed either by law or by love.

Most people, and especially those who are striving to respond to God's call, find that they are guided by a constantly shifting mix of law and love, of fear and trust.

Disadvantages of Law

A person whose actions are always, or at least the greater part of the time, governed by law, whose ideal of what is right or wrong is merely the law, is not very humane. Such a person's life is basically dominated by fear, fear of punishment by God, the police, parents or authority figures. This person tends to turn inward, concentrating on his or her own rectitude in regard to precepts, rather than looking outward to the needs of others.

Jesus told of the two men who went up to the Temple to pray. One whose main concern was to keep the law thought only of himself—of the reward he deserved. The other, who trusted and loved God, looked outward and humbly placed himself in the hands of God *(Luke 18:9–14)*.

The person who lives primarily by the law is one who is controlled, manipulated, or coerced by something or someone outside. Such a person does not enjoy the full freedom of the children of God. More than that, this person tends to restrict the freedom of others to develop and to grow. Such a person tries to mold, manipulate, and coerce others into being the kind of people he or she wants them to be.

Questions
- Why do I need more than law in my life?
- What can I do to expand love and trust in my life?
- What difficulties may I encounter in trying to be a more loving and trusting person?
- What help do I have in becoming a more loving and trusting person?

More Than Law

Law can stifle a creative approach to life. It is written to meet one set of circumstances. It cannot predict or make provisions for every circumstance or for change. Love, on the other hand, provides a more flexible, more creative and a more demanding approach to situations because it tries to take into consideration the needs of the individuals involved as well as the general principles which guide humane Christian response to a situation.

Love and the consequent growth in trust increases when a person follows the same process we see at work in the life of Jesus.

1. Jesus did what he could to help those in need—the physically sick, the psychologically wounded, the sinners.

2. He did more than merely help them, he empathized with them, and he understood their sufferings, failures, and weaknesses to such a degree that Paul could say that Jesus took them all on himself.

3. Because he identified with the needy and the outcasts, Jesus was never judgmental, not even of a close friend who betrayed him to death.

Therefore, if we want to grow in love and trust, we need to foster in ourselves certain attitudes and goals.

1. To strive more and more to help those in physical, psychological, or spiritual need.

2. To recognize and accept our own weaknesses, failures, sins and faults so we can identify with the lowly and the oppressed, so that our service is genuine and not judgmental.

3. To give ourselves and others the benefit of the doubt.

4. To reach out to others with encouragement for them to take hold of their own lives.

5. To respect the differences in people, even in small ways, and to refrain from taking away their own sense of dignity and responsibility.

On the other hand, we *do* strive to take responsibility for our own actions, not pushing it off on others—the Church, God, or other people. We keep in mind that weakness, failure, and the tendency to fear are part of us. When we are acting out of these, we need not indulge in destructive self-criticism.

Difficulties

As I strive to become a more loving and trusting person, I may well find within myself tendencies towards one of the following:

    1. *A messianic complex.* The idea that I have to be perfect and to make everything and everyone else perfect too. It is a temptation to "play God" in regard to myself and others, to "straighten everyone out."

    2. *Cowardliness.* I may be afraid to let go and be led by faith—afraid to trust in the goodness of God and in the fundamental goodness of myself and others. This fear can incline me to cling to what is familiar and secure or to shrink from new possibilities which may require change and responsibility. I may be strongly inclined to rationalize this kind of cowardice and call it prudence.

    3. *Scrupulosity.* The nagging need to be *absolutely* sure of the utter rectitude of all my decisions and actions or to be *exceptionally* correct in my views. Scrupulosity involves an unwillingness to relax and rest in the goodness and mercy of God. Such scrupulosity impels me to strive for a total, complete good which is impossible to achieve rather than to try for that partial or incomplete good which it is possible to attain. One who is driven by this kind of scrupulosity is preoccupied with fear of damnation and is rigid and moralistic towards himself or herself and others.

Helps

As I strive to develop a morality based on love and trust, I can find help in reminding myself of my genuine *desire* to live in this way. I *do* have faith in Jesus. I *have* accepted his offer of salvation. I can reinforce this desire and activate my faith by reading Scripture and reflecting on it. The Scripture will remind me of how Jesus walked humbly with God and showed mercy towards his fellow human beings. I can find strength and encouragement from prayer and from participation in the Eucharist. In moments of prayer I can remind myself of saving events in my life—times when God came to me, saved me from myself, or freed me from fear of failure or outside threats. Even failure can have a positive effect if I use it as an opportunity to reflect on how I came to fail—by giving into legalism, worldliness, cynicism, etc. Such reflection can serve to guide me from the future when such problems might present themselves once again.

Finally, I can deepen my association with a community of people who have the same ideal I have and so will encourage me in my efforts. If I fail, at least some in the community will understand and not be judgmental as they try to help me and strengthen me in my efforts to do better next time.

THE CHRISTIAN COMMUNITY

The Church is a society—a community of people. As such, it must constantly struggle with a tension between fear and trust. It must have rules which keep community order and make it possible for people to grow. At the same time, it should promote the freedom of the individual.

This tension is quite pronounced in the Church. Recent synods of bishops have moved away from the legalistic approach and have called for a more pastoral approach to questions of Church laws and regulations. However, the tension between fear and trust, law and freedom, can be seen in the official documents of the Church and in the approach of bishops, priests and pope to the practical problems of order within the Church. At times, there is a rigorous application of the law and a strong emphasis on the penalties for its violation, an effort to "bring the people into line" by making more laws. But at the same time, in different circumstances and even in the same circumstances but in different times or places, there is a great respect for the freedom of the individual and trust in the ability of the members of the community to work out problems.

The same obstacles which stand in the way of each individual Christian to understand and internalize law also stand in the way of the community's growth from law to freedom, from fear to trust. When these obstacles are faced and dealt with in a humane way, the community, as a community, grows in the one great command of the New Testament, "Love one another as I have loved you" *(John 15:12)*.

PERSONAL PROFILE

Adult Christians are called on to do many diverse things in the course of a day. How open and free are we to respond to the expected and unexpected things which come our way each day? This profile can help you to reflect on some of the real events in your life, to put them into the context of prayer, and to discover how duty and love can be celebrated and enhanced.

Review

Every day is divided into a mixture of *have to's* and *want to's*. This review exercise is designed to help you see how you feel about things in your daily routine—playing tennis, earning a living, cooking, spending time with the children, housework. Any of these things can be perceived and done through either a sense of duty (law) or a sense of caring (love). First, review your past two days (48 hours). Then, make a list of how you spent your time and how long each activity took. Finally, indicate whether the activity was a *duty* activity or a *caring* activity.

Activities	Time	Duty	Caring

Now add up your duty time and your caring time. What do the two figures tell you? Is there a balance between duty time and caring time? Finally, list some changes you would like to see in your life in regard to your approach to daily demands.

1. _____   3. _____

2. _____   4. _____

Prayer

Saint Matthew's Gospel speaks to us regarding both the need to do one's duty and the need to care for self and others. Jesus honored both the law and love in his life. He had priorities for each. Christians today have priorities. We need to examine and measure our priorities of duty, of caring, and of play against the priorities of Jesus. The parables of Jesus as related by Matthew are helpful in our reflections and prayers. Pick one or more of the parables to help you decide your life priorities.

● *Matthew 13:4–12*. Parable of the seed.

● *Matthew 13:44–46*. The buried treasure and the pearl.

● *Matthew 18:21–35*. The official with no mercy.

● *Matthew 20:1–16*. The workers in the vineyard.

● *Matthew 25:1–13*. The ten virgins—the duty of being alert and prepared.

Saint Paul in his letter to the Romans exhorts us to rely on and trust in God, not to place our trust only in law. Ultimately, Jesus is the one who faces and guides us. Select one of the following passages for your reflection and prayer.

● *Romans 5:1–11*. We boast about our faith and hope in God, not in our observance of the law.

● *Romans 8:18–27*. We live in hope. The Spirit prays within us.

● *Romans 8:35–39*. No one, nothing can separate us from the love of God that comes to us in Jesus Christ.

● *Romans 12:9–21*. Our love must be sincere in the service of others; be generous and wholehearted in your service of others.

Preview

Each family celebrates together in different and special ways. Some families come together from all over town to celebrate a special day. Other families celebrate quietly and without joining in with scattered members of the family. Some families have special customs which are repeated from year to year. Other families plan each celebration from scratch. Some celebrations go beyond the boundaries of family into the world of friends and associates. On the first chart below, list family celebrations which are important to you and the manner in which these celebrations are carried out. On the second chart, record celebrations which reach beyond the boundaries of your family and describe the manner of celebration.

Celebrations in the Family	How Celebrated

Celebrations outside the Family	How Celebrated

11 Jesus Calls Us to Celebrate

"This calls for a celebration!" We hear it often. We say it often. It's an instinctive reaction whenever something really good happens—an important anniversary, a family reunion, an achievement or success of one kind or another. We celebrate our very existence on our birthday, that of our nation on the Fourth of July, our friendship and the joy we have in each other in a reunion of friends.

So it isn't at all surprising that we have such celebrations in our faith life. The early Christians were profoundly conscious of the presence of the risen Christ in their midst, especially when they came together to celebrate the Eucharist. He had promised, "Where two or three are gathered in my name, there am I in their midst" *(Matthew 18:20)*. They recognized and celebrated his presence when they gathered in faith to welcome newcomers into the community, to forgive those who had sinned, to pray for the sick members of the community, to witness the marriages of members of the community, and for other purposes. These events were most often celebrated in conjunction with the Eucharist. As time went on, the Church concluded that there were seven basic celebrations which we call sacraments: Eucharist, Baptism, Confirmation, Penance, Anointing of the Sick, Matrimony, and Holy Orders.

Just as there is a difference between celebrations such as a birthday party and an initiation, so there is a difference in the way we celebrate the various sacraments. In every sacrament, as in every celebration, a ritual of some sort is involved. The ritual varies from sacrament to sacrament, just as it does from secular celebration to secular celebration. The words used in the ritual express its fundamental meaning. A cake with twenty-five candles could be used at a twenty-fifth wedding anniversary or a twenty-fifth birthday. It is only when the guests sing "Happy Birthday" or congratulate the couple that we know what the celebration is about. The action of anointing with oil, for example, is used in four sacraments, Baptism, Confirmation, Holy Orders, and the Anointing of the Sick, and it is the words that tell us the purpose in each case.

The ritual of the sacraments is much more than a few essential words and an action. It encompasses all the prayers and ceremonies which celebrate a specific faith-event. A person graduates from high school by satisfactorily completing a designated course of studies, but graduation is enhanced, made more memorable and important by a prom, a procession, caps and gowns, speeches, diplomas. The Church over the centuries has put together a ritual comprising many prayers and ceremonies to express what is happening at one point in the life of a believer and in the life of the community of believers. Not all these actions and prayers are essential, but they give richness and depth of meaning to what is happening. For example, the essential ritual of pouring water and saying, "I baptize you in the name of the Father and of the Son and of the Holy Spirit" is all that is absolutely necessary for Baptism, but the presence of a sponsor, the questioning and the profession of faith, the Scripture readings, the homily, and the prayers of petition all emphasize the acceptance of the person into the community of believers. The presentation of the lighted candle, the putting on of a white garment, the anointing with oil, and the prayers make more clear that the person is resolved to live in a new way.

The sacraments are not merely ritual. Even the most elaborate and beautiful ritual is merely show or entertainment without a deep faith on the part of those who participate in the celebration. Faith looks beyond what is said and done to grasp the unseen and mysterious activity of Christ in our lives. If faith is not present, the celebration would be little more than ritualistic mumbo-jumbo or a mere cultural observance, smacking more of custom and habit than of spiritual significance. Faith helps us realize that the risen Christ is indeed present whenever we come together in his name.

Faith-filled ritual also makes us conscious that in the celebration of the sacraments he is present in a very special way. We perform the ritual in reverent awareness of who we are and what we are doing. The risen Christ is present with his Spirit, validating and making effective the realities celebrated.

Questions
- **Why do we need ritual to express our faith life?**
- **What events in our faith life do we celebrate in the sacraments?**

Need for Ritual

We need ritual to pinpoint, highlight, publicly express, and share with others the significant events of our faith-life. For the most part, the movement of God in our lives and our struggles to respond go on in the depths of our being. We have to bring them out into the open and celebrate them in a ritual for ourselves and for others to see and rejoice in them. The important events of our faith life usually occur over a period of time. Seldom do they happen all at once. Often we are not too conscious of what is occurring or perceive it only in a confused way. The celebration of the sacraments pulls together and expresses clearly what has been going on in our faith-life.

Baptism

As we have seen, the process of conversion involves time and a psychological process. By being baptized we publicly profess that we have received a call from God, that we are willing to accept it. We proclaim that we will try to lead a life of love and service as exemplified by Jesus. We also acknowledge that we need the help of other believers in living this life. The community of believers, in turn, accepts our commitment to the Christian way of life and pledges to help us lead the new life.

We publicly embrace this new life of faith by Baptism. Baptism summons us to see ourselves, our society, and our destiny not merely in terms of our culture, our politics, or our social position but also in terms of the Gospel. Baptism involves the hidden and mysterious workings of the Holy Spirit, helping us put together a life-style which embodies care and concern for as well as empathy and identity with the weak, the suffering, and the oppressed.

Infants cannot make this type of public commitment. When infants are baptized, the parents, godparents, and the community are committing themselves to give guidance and example to the child so that the child will someday want to make the commitment his or her own. A person baptized as an infant makes this commitment later, either by a conscious, explicit decision or by an implicit decision contained in living a life permeated and guided by faith.

Confirmation

The call of God is not merely one of personal growth and salvation. It involves a mission to do what we can to help others free themselves from the things which hinder them from becoming the best kind of human beings they can become. In Confirmation, whether it is celebrated years after Baptism or as part of one's initiation into the Church, we publicly affirm our acceptance of that mission and of our need for God's help in carrying it out. Through this ritual the risen Christ assures us that the Holy Spirit is with us at all times to strengthen, enlighten, and comfort us in our efforts to fulfill the mission.

Eucharist

At regular intervals we need to stand back and review our progress in becoming the kind of person we are called to be. Our daily lives are so filled with distractions that we need to set time aside to see how well we are doing. We will find that at times we forget who we really are and to what we have been called. We need to be reminded of the faith vision we embraced in Baptism. We may find that we shrink from the difficulties we are facing and do not trust God's promise to be with us. Even if we have succeeded fairly well in our efforts to become a more humane person, we need affirmation as well as forgiveness in our efforts to live the Christian life. This process may, of course, be done privately. But the community regularly celebrates a simple ritual meal which expresses all those needs and promises God's support.

At his Last Supper with his apostles, Jesus told them to break the bread of his body and to share the cup of his blood as a constant memorial of him, of his life, death, resurrection, and ascension. When we share in the Body and Blood of Christ, we are reminded that we are a people called to live as Jesus did. We also have to suffer and die before we achieve final victory. We have to die to our personal weaknesses and selfishness and to our cultural and social identity so that we can live our faith identity—as a child of God, a brother or sister of Jesus, and a friend of the Holy Spirit.

Each time we celebrate the Eucharist with sorrow for our sinfulness God assures us anew of his love and forgiveness. Each time we participate in the Eucharist with a realization of our powerlessness and weakness God is assuring us that his strength is our strength. When we open our minds and our hearts to the readings and to the homily, we signify our desire for help from the Holy Spirit to discern what we have to do day by day to live the faith-life.

The ritual of Eucharist enables us to join our efforts to live a life of faith to those of Jesus and to offer both as a gift to God and a sacrifice of praise and love. In this offering we thank God for all he has done for us.

Finally, by sharing in the Body and Blood of Christ, we show that we live by a faith which sees beyond appearances. We recognize that in some deep mysterious way we are one with Jesus Christ and with one another.

Baptism and Confirmation are sacraments which cannot be repeated. The Eucharist, on the other hand, is so central to the faith life of the community that it is celebrated daily and Catholics are called to participate in it at least weekly.

Penance

As we try to live out our call and mission, we will experience our own woundedness and selfishness. We can be the biggest obstacle in the way of our mission. Faced with our selfishness we can decide whether we are going to try to be in total control or simply surrender to the mystery of God's care.

Either choice can involve sin or failure. If I try to stay in total control, I reject a faith vision of life. If I turn my life over to God with no personal responsibility, I may fail to hear him. In either case I need forgiveness. By participating in the sacrament of Reconciliation I once more affirm that I want to be brought into unity with whom I am called to be—with other people and with God. God, through this ritual of the Church, shows that he is once again accepting my commitment. He is once again promising to help me live a Gospel life-style.

Anointing of the Sick

When I am physically ill, I am to some degree in isolation from family and community because I cannot follow my customary way of living out my Christian commitment. When a sick person is anointed, the community is expressing its care and concern for the person and the person is accepting this concern. The person receiving the anointing is also affirming his or her willingness to accept the change in life-style imposed by illness even though it may involve the ultimate change—death. God is making visible his concern for the total person and is promising that he is with the person even though he or she cannot live a normal life. When the sick person accepts God as present and caring even in sickness, a healing takes place. Sometimes this healing is physical because harmony has been established in the person. At other times the healing is an interior peace which comes from the realization that the sick person can live out the call and mission in a different way than he or she anticipated.

Marriage

Christians live out their commitment to God in many ways. Some decide to live a single life. Others decide to live a life under the vows of poverty, chastity, and obedience. The majority, however, decide to live a married life. When a couple discovers that they love one another enough to wish to commit themselves to each other for life, they make public their commitment by exchanging marriage vows in the presence of the community. The exchange of vows shows what has been going on in their lives and what they hope will continue to go on until death parts them.

If this total life-commitment is not present, if the couple does not realize what is involved in their commitment, or if faith in God and in his activity is missing, then the marriage ceremony is not the celebration of a faith event. Marriage becomes a celebration of faith only when those who enter it realize and accept the call, the mission, and the support of God.

Holy Orders

Although all Christians have the mission of proclaiming God's love and goodness, the community selects some members to proclaim in a special way the call of God for people to become more humane and to grow as human beings.

These people also have the task of reminding the rest of the community of the meaning of the call, especially in the celebration of the Eucharist and the other sacraments. The bishops, the priests, and the deacons are called to comfort the suffering, the weak, and the powerless the same way Jesus did by caring for them and by identifying with them. They are called to remind the oppressors, the powerful, the indifferent, and the negligent that all people are God's children and are to be freed from those restraints, social, economic, political, educational, and physical which keep them from developing as full human beings.

The task of these ordained ministers is to walk with God's people not as leaders lording it over the people but as servants caring for the needs of the people. When they preside, at the liturgy it should be as one member of the family helping brothers and sisters express their faith experience in ritual. When they teach, it should be as fellow pilgrims sharing the pain and joy of the journey. When they direct the community, it should be as caring servants such as Jesus was to his disciples.

Questions
 ● **What problems make it difficult for people to celebrate the sacraments as faith events in their lives?**
 ● **How can we make our involvement in the sacraments more meaningful?**

Problems

The problems which make it difficult for people to celebrate the sacraments as real faith experiences come from two sources—those which arise from our own attitudes and ideas and those which come from outside us. Some of the internal problems are the following:

1. *Impatience with the notion of signs and symbols.* Some have the attitude that such things are fanciful

and unreal, that they have no place in the practical affairs of everyday life.

2. *Superstition*. Some tend to regard the sacraments as magical signs which will work independently of faith and intention.

3. *Routine*. It can happen that one grows so accustomed to a sacrament (especially Penance and Eucharist) that it becomes a matter of habit, and one approaches the sacrament passively and with little thought.

4. *Individualism*. If we regard the sacraments as purely personal encounters with the risen Christ and are oblivious of their relationship with the community, we can fail to grasp the reality of our union with others in and through Christ.

5. *Improper motivation*. If we approach the sacraments without faith, merely from a desire to conform to the expectations of our family or our culture, we fail to benefit from the sacraments as we could. People who have a church wedding to please mother or because it is expected but who themselves are not believers or involved in any way with the Christian community's activities could fall into this category.

The main problem outside ourselves which makes it difficult for us to enter into and get the most benefit from the sacraments is a mechanical, lifeless, or poorly presented liturgy. If the celebrant does not understand the role of leader and truly communicate with the people or if the celebrant merely goes through the actions and words in a hasty or thoughtless way, people find it hard to realize what the ritual is celebrating. The congregation can be just as big a problem. If the people do not participate with faith and fervor in the prayers, singing, and actions, it is difficult for an individual to be aware of the sacredness and meaning of the sacrament being celebrated.

An Attitude of Celebration

In the last analysis, however, our participation in the sacraments depends on our own attitudes. A good celebrant, a well-planned liturgy, and an enthusiastic congregation can help us in our efforts to celebrate a faith-event. But even if none of these is present, the liturgy can be meaningful to us if in deep faith we realize what is happening.

We can make our involvement with the sacraments more meaningful by preparing ourselves with reflection and prayer beforehand and by striving to apply the grace and strength we gain from the sacraments in our daily lives.

Any celebration is more or less effective depending on the seriousness with which we approach it and enter into it. The better we prepare to meet the risen Christ in the sacraments the more clearly we understand what we are about, and the more open and receptive we are, the more effective our encounter with him will be. The better we follow it up by subsequent behavior, the more effective will be our future celebrations. As with any meaningful human relationship, the more frequently and intimately we encounter the risen Christ in the sacraments, the deeper and more meaningful will be all our encounters with him.

THE CHRISTIAN COMMUNITY

The reform of the rites of the sacraments by Vatican Council II has helped to make their meaning and their social nature clearer.

In Baptism, the emphasis is on re-birth into the Christian community and, in the case of infant baptism, the responsibility of parents and godparents. Instead of the emphasis being merely on remission of sin, it is on membership in the community and the living of the Christian life within that community.

The same renewal of emphasis is to be found in the

sacrament of Reconciliation, wherein the idea of reconciliation with the community is stressed and the rite is performed at times in a communal setting. The same is true of the Anointing of the Sick. This sacrament is most ideally celebrated with the community.

More and more, Confirmation is being celebrated when those who are confirmed are old enough to understand what the sacrament means and to appreciate the responsibilities it entails.

At the time of the Reformation, when the efficacy of the sacraments was called into question, the teaching Church laid great stress on the fact that the sacraments have their effect whenever they are celebrated validly—with proper intention and the necessary signs and symbols and with no obstacle placed in the way by those who take part in the sacrament. Such emphasis at times gave rise to a somewhat mechanical administration and reception of the sacraments. The Council replaced this stress with a greater emphasis on the necessity of meaningful celebration. The Council also encouraged those who partake of the sacraments to grow in their attitude of communal celebration.

PERSONAL PROFILE

The sacraments are part of our identity as Catholic Christians. They call us to celebrate God's love and care for us. We enter into the celebration of the sacraments with the awareness of who we are and how we choose to live. It is important to reinforce the value of sacraments in our lives by reflecting on special moments which we have experienced. It is important, too, to search the Scripture for a deeper understanding of celebration. Use this opportunity to put your memory and your imagination to work to foster a deeper appreciation for the sacraments.

Review

The Eucharist reminds us weekly at the Sunday celebration that we belong to God. Make a list of times during your last celebration of the Eucharist when you recalled or renewed your faith. Describe the moment and the effect it had on you.

Parts of the Mass that remind me I am God's	Effect these parts of the Mass have on me

The readings during the Eucharist also remind us to live lives of love and of service to others. Briefly describe a homily or sermon which had an effect on you.

(NOTE: This should be a reading or homily you experienced in the context of a sacramental celebration.)

_____

_____

_____

Prayer

Celebrating the goodness of God is an important part of our faith life. We are called upon to celebrate the gift of our faith, the gift of Christ in our life, and the gift of sharing our faith, hope, and love with others. These passages from Saint Paul exhort us to rejoice, to give thanks, and to express our praise to God. Select one of these passages to reflect upon your call to celebrate God's goodness to you.

● *Philippians 4:4–9.* The call to praise, to rejoice.

● *Colossians 3:12–17.* The call to thanksgiving with song.

● *Ephesians 3:14–21.* Paul prays for his readers and gives glory to God.

● *Ephesians 6:18–20.* Pray for one another.

The Eucharist is a meal ritual. Food represents life and love to people. God fed his people in the desert with water, manna, and quail. Jesus is the bread of life. Our Father nourishes and sustains our spirit-life in the Eucharist. Select one of the Scripture passages below and ponder how the Father nourishes and sustains you, your life.

● *Psalm 78:20–29.* Food for the journeying Israelites in the desert.

● *John 6:26–51.* Jesus is the bread of life.

● *I Corinthians 11:23–34.* Paul exhorts the people to participate in the Lord's Supper with care.

Preview

Many times in the course of our lifetime each of us asks, "Who am I?" There are many ways to answer that question. Sometimes we define ourselves in relation to the roles we assume or are given in life. Sometimes we define ourselves in terms of our characteristics. Check off on the lists below the phrases which best tell who you are.

The individual me:

___ the shy one	___ the peaceful one	___ the failure
___ the angry one	___ the joyful one	___ the bright one
___ the bold one	___ the optimist	___ the dull one
___ the emotional one	___ the pessimist	___ the artistic one
___ the steady one	___ the lazy one	___ the neat one
___ the loner	___ the fighter	___ the peaceful one
___ the up-tight one	___ the free one	___ the questioning one
___ other _____	___ other _____	___ other _____

The social me:

___ daughter	___ husband	___ single woman
___ son	___ aunt	___ enemy
___ mother	___ uncle	___ acquaintance

___ father   ___ grandparent   ___ loner

___ sister   ___ in-law relative ___ stepparent

___ brother   ___ friend   ___ divorced person

___ wife   ___ bachelor   ___ separated
                                            person

___ other _____   ___ other _____   ___ other _____

The worker or business me:

___ I work for myself   ___ I work in a factory

___ I work for another   ___ I work in an office

___ I work at home   ___ I am in a service
                                industry
___ I am retired
                            ___ I am in entertainment
___ I am in management
                            ___ I am in manufacturing
___ I am the boss of my
company   ___ I am a professional

___ I work with my hands   ___ I belong to a labor
                                organization
___ I work primarily with
my head   ___ other_____

___ I am in the trades   ___ other_____

_____

_____

Jesus Calls Us to a Faith Community

"Are you somebody?" The question was asked of the wife of a prominent politician as she registered for a room in a hotel. The woman was upset by the question. Yes, as the wife of a well-known man, she was somebody in that sense. But, apart from her social position, wasn't she somebody in a more basic, more radical sense? And what about other people, she wondered, people who were not rich or famous or well-connected? The upshot was that the woman wrote a book entitled *Everybody is Somebody*.

Is everybody somebody? Am I really somebody? Basically and radically, apart from the accidentals, the externals, who am I, and what am I worth? These are questions which occur to thoughtful persons at some time or other in some way or other.

Such questions as these may have arisen in the minds of the two unimportant fishermen who were walking along the bank of the river Jordan nearly two thousand years ago. From a socio-economic aspect they were nobodies. But after Philip and James had spent the day with Jesus they had a new sense of who and what they were. Through Jesus they had received a call from God. As they responded to that call they began to realize that they were unique personalities, cherished by God and summoned to an important mission. Thus it was that these future apostles began to see and understand their core identity—children of God, brothers of

Jesus Christ, destined to live forever. Their reaction was to seek out others with whom they could share the good news of their discovery.

This is the way it is with every person who responds to the call of God. As I respond I acquire a new understanding of my core identity, a new realization of who I am—a unique person, loved and valued by God, called to a special mission to work for his kingdom, and destined for eternal life. With this new discovery I inevitably seek the company and support of others who have the same understanding of their identity and mission. I realize that it is only in community with others that I can grow, receive strength for my weakness and woundedness, and engage in the mission we all have to serve others and build the kingdom of God.

This is the origin of Church. Too often we still tend to think of Church in terms of an institution, a bureaucracy, buildings, authority figures, laws, and regulations—all sorts of things which are large, impersonal, and outside ourselves. Too often, we think that membership in the Church is a matter of "going along" with what I was born into. I may have been baptized into the Church as an infant and raised in it. I may think of joining the Church as I would join a club or political party I believe in or become a citizen of a country I choose as my own.

Actually, while the Church is a visible body, an institution, and an external organization, it is much more basically people. It is people who recognize their special call, realize their core identity and unite to worship together, support, serve, and minister to one another. It is people who seek strength for their weakness and engage in their mission—to work for the kingdom of God.

The kingdom is made up of those who accept the call of God to become the most fully human persons they can become. The call of God helps these people realize that even with all their limitations, faults, and sins they are loved and cherished by God. More than that, accepting God's call with faith gives them the assurance that their own personal uniqueness will never be destroyed. It assures them that in the life after life they will continue to be the one of a kind individual they are now. This faith-vision assures these people that their ultimate value, identity, and destiny are determined not by family, wealth, power, or talents but by the fact that they are the *People of God.*

And it is here that Church becomes inevitable. Such a realization impels those who have accepted the call to acknowledge it publicly and join the others who share the same faith-vision. Thus the community of believers comes into being. It is a community which realizes that the Spirit of Jesus lives and acts in them as a group and in the individual members. The presence and activity of the Spirit is manifested by the fact that they try, as Jesus did, to minister to others and call others to such a faith identity.

The members of the Church community try to serve others in a selfless way. They try to accept and identify with the weak and the sinful rather than judging and criticizing them. They try to be present to others who are in need. Living according to the Spirit of the risen Christ involves a constant process of dying to self and a constant rising to a new and different life.

This is the Gospel ideal, the Christian ideal, and the Catholic ideal. As such it is something more striven for than attained. It is an ideal which does come to realization in various degrees in the lives of individual members of the Church. The Church as a whole, even with all the faults which are so painfully evident, is nonetheless striving to measure up to this ideal.

There are faults, weaknesses (even glaring ones), scandals (even large ones), inconsistencies, and even contradictions in the life of the Church and its members. Even though the Church is a People, it is at the same time a huge and cumbersome institution and is subject to the weaknesses which beset human institutions. Nonetheless, the Church is a People who are struggling to achieve and keep alive this different sense of self—a self not determined by family, power, or culture. It is a People who continually struggle with the meaning of their mission.

Whenever the Church has been at all successful in living up to the ideal, it has been because it identified with the poor, the needy, the sick, and the suffering. The Church has ministered to the nobodies of society and tried to help them realize their value and their true identity. In such cases, the Church has been a vital force in the lives of individuals and in society—a force for freedom and justice. When it has been untrue to its mission and has identified with rich and powerful vested interests or has allowed itself to become an establishment, it has been a force for repression and injustice. But, even with the ups and downs, the advances and retrogressions that have marked the pages of its long history, the Church has always continued the struggle to reform and renew itself—to realign itself to its mission. Even in the darkest periods of the Church's history, when there was widespread·corruption, there were always deeply spiritual, thoroughly Christian members of the Church who lived lives filled with the ideals of the Church. In the midst of sin and weakness, they gave themselves wholeheartedly to the Church's mission.

What has been said above about the discovery of core identity and the sense of a mission to work for the kingdom of God applies to all the Christian Churches within the Church in its wider sense. Catholics see the Catholic Church as the central body—the one in which the kingdom subsists more fully, with the sacramental rites, particularly the Eucharistic Celebration, with the unbroken line of episcopal succession dating back to the apostles, with the strong bond of unity which is centered in the pope as the visible head of the Church. Catholics also enjoy the emphasis on traditions which have been established throughout the centuries. Catholics also experience a great family structure within the Catholic community—an emphasis on our fellowship with the saints and particularly with Mary, the mother of Jesus. She is given a special place within the communion of saints.

Within the Catholic Church there is a great sense of authority and unity, but there is also a truly remarkable diversity—one which belies the image of a strictly monolithic organization that many have of the Catholic Church. From country to country, Roman Catholicism has a strikingly different flavor. Contrary to what many think and expect, there are many different theologies, theological schools, and opinions within the Catholic Church. There are many different liturgies and rites in many different languages, there are many different disciplines—clerical celibacy in the western rites and a married clergy in the eastern rites within the Church. In short, what Roman Catholics cherish in the Catholic Church is, on the one hand, the security they find in the strong emphasis on tradition, authority, and unity and, on the other, the amazing differences which are part of that universal character which gives it the name of Catholic.

Questions
- **How do people relate to the Catholic Church?**
- **How is this relationship manifested?**

How People Relate to the Church

Those Catholics who have strong positive feelings about the Church relate to it in a vital, energetic, meaningful way. They are proud of their membership, feel good about being Catholic and see themselves as striving to become better persons because they belong to the Church. They see the Church as a vital and essential part of their lives. They affirm that God has a vital place in their lives and show this faith by joining in the community prayer life, by some form of private prayer life and by helping the needy.

People with a strong positive feeling about the Church look to it to give meaning and direction to their lives. They find comfort, stability and security in being a member of the People of God. Some of this group realize that they make up the Church. They value the tradition, the practices, and the structure of the Church. At the same time, they weigh the official policies, teachings, and positions of the Church and tend to judge them in the light of their experience and background. They feel that they can contribute something to the insights, the practices, the decisions, the teachings of the Church. Many of those who experience the Church in this way are concerned with being more active in the life, worship and ministry of the Church and are eager to assume more responsibility.

The fact that people relate in a strong way to the Church does not mean that they do not have questions, periods of doubts, difficulties, and struggles with the Church. These difficulties surface most strongly when people reevaluate their own image of and relationship to the Church. For example, early in life people usually see the Church as something separate from themselves. They see it as a parent, a teacher, a law-giver, and a power-figure. They see their role primarily as one of submission to authority. Later in life, especially when they establish their own self-identity as a Christian, they may begin to see the Church as a community of fellow believers and their relationship as mainly one of mutual trust, respect, and support. When this shift takes place, all sorts of internal and external tensions, struggle and confusion arise.

These tensions and difficulties occur because the people see the Church in a different way or because the Church begins to act in a different way. For example, the people who at one time looked to the Church as a parent, an infallible teacher, a law-giver supreme begin to feel tension and have problems when they come to see the Church as a community of believers which does not have all the answers and is struggling with the same problems. They begin to feel that the infallible teacher restricts their freedom to find the truth, that the law-giver has become a mere legalist, and that the parent is a domineering parent. On the other hand, some people experience tension and struggle because they want a parent, infallible teacher, and law-giver. They find the Church shifting to collegial models of acting, to a pastoral rather than a legalistic approach, and to greater openness to divergent opinions.

When shifts such as these occur, people feel at a loss. Often they become angry, cynical, or bitter. They may even attack or hate the Church. But these negative reactions show a vital *feeling* relationship to the Church.

In this disillusionment, these people are actually receiving a call from God to grow in their individual potential. If they accept the call and take the time and effort to work through their new images and relationships with the Church, they can move into a deeper more vital and satisfying relationship with the People of God.

There is another group of people, whether Catholic or not, who have no vital relationship to the Church. They have little or no feeling either way. Many people who profess to be Catholic fall into this category. They can't think of themselves as anything but Catholic, but being Catholic has little or no effect on what they think or do. They do not react one way or the other to issues raised by the Church. They may go to Mass now and then, want to be married in the Church and buried from it, but somehow they have missed making a radical faith commitment.

Questions
- **What are some of the different models or images of Church people have which cause these problems?**
- **What are some of the advantages and disadvantages of each of these models?**

Models

Many of the negative feelings people have about Church and the tensions they experience with Church come from the fact that people have in their minds a model or ideal of Church. That model or ideal is seldom realized to their satisfaction. The Church is a very complex institution. It is impossible to describe in a few paragraphs what it is or what it does for people. Basically, it tries to meet the varying needs of many people. Jesus told the apostles to preach the good news to all people, and people are different in every age and place.

Father Avery Dulles says that there are at least five generic or basic models of the Church. It is easy to see that a person can become angry, frustrated, or simply "turned off" if he or she holds to one model and has to live with a community which operates on another. All the models or images of Church contain essential elements of the true and full Christian life. But each person, each community will tend to emphasize one more than the others.

Some people see the Church primarily as *herald*. The People of God are gathered and formed by Scripture and their primary mission is to proclaim God's Word and to move people to put their faith in Jesus as Lord and Saviour. Those who emphasize this model will be zealous in bringing people into the Church. They can, however, easily give simplistic or fundamental explanations of Scripture and oversimplify the process of conversion and salvation. Rather than insisting on deeds in the social and public areas of life as a sign of real conversion, they can easily be satisfied with mere professions of salvation.

Others see the Church as *servant*. They build their lives around their efforts to transform society and infuse it with the values of the kingdom. Without people who hold this vision, the Church could easily become so "other worldly" that it would never touch social institutions. But they become discouraged when all Christians—especially the leaders of the Church—do not join the good causes they espouse. They easily fall into the trap of thinking that the only really important thing for a Christian to do is to change social institutions and to do this they may too easily adopt uncritically the tactics and weapons of the world they are trying to change.

A segment of the Christian community sees the Church primarily as *sacrament,* or *sign*. The People of God come into being through prayer and worship and they are a sign to the world of the presence of Christ and of the hope for redemption which he promises. They can, however, become so concerned with the aesthetic aspects of the liturgy that it loses its vitality. They run the risk of ignoring the evils in the world because they are so wrapped up in contemplation.

Today a great many people see the Church primarily as *community,* people united to God and to one another in love. Without love there is no community, no real support, no affirmation. Community cannot be sought, it must happen. People who operate on this model may run from group to group seeking exciting religious experiences and warm relationships. Exciting liturgies, warm relationships, and close family feelings are impossible to find on a large scale in a Church which has great numbers of members from different social and cultural groups. Such a community can only be held together by ritual and ties which at times seem cold and impersonal because they must blend together so many different groups.

Finally, there are those who are most comfortable seeing the Church as an *institution,* as a structured community built around a pastoral office endowed with authority to teach, to guide, and to preside over the liturgy. This view is absolutely necessary to give order, coherence, and continuity to the Church, but it can lead to rigidity, conformity, and a doctrinaire attitude which makes an idol of church structure. This view can also lead to a division in the community which sees the leaders as *the* Church—as being solely responsible for the direction the Church takes and the rest of the faithful merely as sheep to be led.

Each person will construct his or her own image of Church *which will be authentic only in as far as it combines, to different degrees, all five models.* The institutional image or model, while necessary, should not be the primary model or image. It should always be seen as the tool or means God has given his people to be *heralds, servants, family,* and *signs of his presence.*

THE CHRISTIAN COMMUNITY

In the past the answer to the question "Why should I be Catholic?" was given in terms of "good guys" and "bad guys." The Catholic Church was one, holy, catholic, and apostolic. The other Churches were not. These simple answers are not so convincing today. Each person has to come to his or her own conclusion as to what the community of Catholics offers him or her. The diversity and flexibility which exists in the Catholic Church appeals to some. Others are enchanted by its unity and stability. The beauty and scope of its liturgy; the fullness of its doctrine; the apostolic tradition of its hierarchy; the works of charity; its tolerance of sinners; its survival in face of triumphalism, pride, ambition, and worldly maneuvering; all these are convincing and appealing realities.

In any case my becoming or remaining a Catholic should result from the realization that I am accepting a gift which God offers me and that this gift meets certain needs I have. I do not join the Catholic Church as I would join a club but I accept the invitation from God to grow as a person—to become the person he wants me to be within the community of those who embrace Roman Catholicism. Becoming Catholic even though I happen to be one should satisfy my need for a clearer realization of what the faith vision implies—a need for challenge, security, and the freedom to grow in my own individual manner.

Even though the Catholic vision of the faith-life is not perfect or complete and is marred by weakness and imperfection for Catholics, it does seem to have among all religions and denominations the most comprehensive and most balanced expression of *belief* (creed), of *worship* (cult) and of *ethics* (code). This combination of creed, cult and code has been developing for two thousand years under the influence of vastly different cultures, political systems and economic situations and, while far from perfect, it seems to committed Catholics to be the best and most complete expression of the kingdom of God that we have.

The Catholic Church also offers us tremendous possibilities of developing a faith-life in our own personal and unique way. Because so many different streams of human activity and culture, East and West, rich and poor, ancient and modern, flow together in the Catholic Church we find in it great diversity in unity. We find all forms of prayer available, from the charismatic prayer groups to the highly individualized journeying into the depths of one's own being. We find a great variety of opportunities to serve, console, and comfort the needy. We find many streams of thought, from Greek logic to French existentialism, as well as very difficult faith visions, all existing side by side in the Catholic Church.

This variety in the Church militates against perfect harmony and peace, but it does give people the opportunity to grow and to help one another grow by sharing different visions and options. At times, people may get hurt in pursuing one or the other faith-vision but on the whole the Catholic Church embraces or at least tolerates an astonishing variety of ways in which people can express their faith-vision.

I can find security and stability in the Catholic Church which has maintained its identity for two thousand years. This security and stability does not imply that change is not constantly occurring, but it does imply that the changes will be solid when they do occur. An ancient world-wide community takes its time in sorting out the meaning of what God is saying through the experience of people. The process of discernment is slower but more valid than changes based on the prevalent fashions of thought or culture.

The greatest security and stability comes from the fact that good numbers of people through the ages have tried to make present the spirit of Christ in their lives. This effort indicates that there is something true and stable at the core of the Catholic faith. This core can be seen in every age in the lives of those Catholics who have shown remarkable faith, hope, and loving care for others. The fact that some people do not live this core does not mean that I cannot find the presence of the Holy Spirit in the Catholic community to bring me into faith and hope.

No matter what motivates me to become Catholic and to remain Catholic, within the Catholic community I will find my rich spiritual heritage and religious identity. It will be within this community that I will have to assume responsibility and place my unique talents at the disposal of the community members. Saint Paul said it well to the Corinthians twenty centuries ago.

The body is one and has many members, but all the members, many though they are, are one body; and so it is with Christ. It was in one Spirit that all of us, whether Jew or Greek, slave or free, were baptized into one body. All of us have been given to drink of the one Spirit. Now the body is not one member, it is many. If the foot should say, "Because I am not a hand I do not belong to the body," would it then no longer belong to the body? If the ear should say, "Because I am not an eye I do not belong to the body," would it then no longer belong to the body? If the body were all eye, what would happen our hearing? If it were all ear, what would happen to our smelling? As it is, God has set each member of the body in the place he wanted it to be. If all the members were alike, where would the body be? There are, indeed, many different members, but one body. The eye cannot say to the hand, "I do not need you," any more than the head can say to the feet, "I do not need you." Even those members of the body which seem less important are in fact indispensable. We honor the members we consider less honorable by clothing them with greater care, thus bestowing on the less presentable a propriety which the more presentable already have. God has so constructed the body as to give greater honor to the lowly members, that there may be no dissension in the body, but that all the members may be concerned for one another. If one member suffers, all the members suffer with it; if one member is honored, all the members share its joy.

You, then are the body of Christ. Every one of you is a member of it. Furthermore, God has set up in the Church first apostles, second prophets, third teachers, then miracle workers, healers, assistants, administrators, and those who speak in tongues. Are all apostles? Are all prophets? Are all teachers? Do all work miracles or have the gift of healing? Do all speak in tongues, all have the gift of interpretation of tongues? Set your hearts on the greater gifts.

(1 Corinthians 12:12–31)

PERSONAL PROFILE

Belonging to the community is of the essence of Catholicism. Many people feel a strong sense of belonging to the Church, but they never take the time to reflect on the experience. There are two ways in which this can be done simply and quickly. The first is to express concretely and to reflect on the model that one is operating on in relation to the Church. The other is to confront God's Word and to pray over one's experience of the Church in the *light of Scripture*. This profile is an opportunity to do both. This profile also leads to an expression of those basic relationships which are part of Christian faith.

Review

You studied the five models of the Church that were presented by Avery Dulles. Review them. Then, describe in two or three words what each model means to you. Finally, rank the models in the order of their importance to you.

Models of Church	Description	Priority
Herald		
Servant		
Sacrament or Sign		
Community		
Institution		

Now reflect on the model you marked as ranking first in importance. Write down in some detail what operating under this model means to you.

_____

_____

_____

_____

_____

_____

Prayer

A mature Christian needs to pray frequently to ask for the trust needed to accept his or her core identity in the Church. The prayers below help to deepen your appreciation of your identity within the community of faith.

● *Matthew 7:7–11.* Our Father's love and care for his children. Trust his care.

- *Matthew 11:28–30.* Learn from Jesus how to be gentle and humble. He refreshes us when we are weary.

- *Mark 3:31–35.* Whoever does the will of God is my brother, my sister, and my mother.

- *Mark 10:13–16.* We are called to accept as a child would the sign of God our Father. We acknowledge that we are his children.

The shared life and vision of the first Christian community are described in the *Acts of the Apostles.* They are presented in an ideal manner. Read one of the following passages and reflect on the portrayal. Then, use your reflection to write summary answers to the two questions which conclude this prayer experience.

- *Acts 2:42–47.*   - *Acts 4:32–35.*

How does your life-style (family life) enter into and resemble the ideal of the first Christians?

_____

_____

_____

How can you improve your sharing in the Christian community life in the context of your own life-style (family life)?

_____

_____

_____

Preview

Family relationships are complex. Yet, we all carry ideals and models of family relationships around in our heads. Fill in the following blanks quickly and spontaneously. Do not think about what the expected answer might be. Simply record the first answers which come into your mind.

1. Fatherhood.

A father is _____

An ideal father is _____

_____

_____

2. Brotherhood.

A brother or sister is _____

An ideal brother or sister is _____

_____

_____

3. Friendship.

A friend is _____

An ideal friend is _____

_____

_____

13 Jesus Calls Us to Union with God

Have you ever been lonely?

Being lonely isn't at all like merely being alone. Being lonely means feeling the pain of isolation, of not having someone to share one's thoughts and feelings with. It means experiencing the emptiness that comes from not having someone to relate to, be challenged by, or learn from.

We have all felt loneliness at times, and we can recall the joy we felt when we found ourselves once more with a really close friend, one whom we love and who loves us. Such a close friend can widen our horizon, open our mind and heart, and enlarge our very self.

This is what a really deep relationship does for us. When we have such a relationship, we grow by coming to understand and even to *share* the thoughts and feelings of the other. We enter into that person's world, think as that person thinks, and feel as that person feels. As we come to know another more intimately and understand him or her better, we come to know and understand ourselves better as well.

This is the way it happens in our *human* relationships. And this is the way it happens, too, in our *relationship with Jesus,* once we have accepted him as our model and Savior, as one who lives now with the fullness of life, and as a vital influence in our life.

180

We cannot fail to be struck by the unique and profound relationship Jesus had with the Father. He had a deep need for human companionship, but deeper still was his need to go off by himself and spend hours and sometimes whole days and nights in conversation with the Father. He spoke of God as no man has ever spoken, using the term *abba,* a word which connotes the deepest trust and intimacy. There is no really exact English equivalent. The closest is the word that only a loving, playful child would use, daddy.

The message that Jesus brought to the people was the joyful news that his Father was their Father as well. In parable after parable, he spoke of God as the loving parent who knows our needs far better than we do ourselves and who cares for us even more than he cares for the beautiful world he created and lovingly sustains and nourishes. He showed the Father as the merciful Father of the prodigal son, the one who never gives up, never loses hope, and never ceases to love—no matter what. Jesus cut through the jungle of legalism and the florid prayers of the Pharisees and taught his followers to pray with confidence and love. Jesus summed it all up in the profound simplicity of the *Our Father.* And Jesus spoke of God also in another way, one which also conveyed the greatest intimacy, care and presence. He himself continually drew strength, consolation, and inspiration from the Spirit who dwelt within him. He promised to send this Spirit to dwell with his followers. The Spirit would be their advocate, friend, and companion. The Spirit would be the abiding presence of Jesus and the Father in the community, giving strength and inspiration and helping the members to strive day-by-day to have the mind and heart of Christ.

Jesus claimed for himself a relationship to the Father so special that after his resurrection, his disciples came to the realization that he deserved the title Lord—a title that Jews gave only to God. Peter said Jesus was "exalted at God's right hand," that "God has made both Lord and Messiah this Jesus whom you crucified" *(Acts 2:33,36).* The disciples believed firmly that Jesus, a man with whom they had lived and worked, was more than a mere man. He was the

Son of God—God among them in some way which is beyond comprehension. Jesus is at the same time fully human and yet fully divine—the only Son of the living God.

By entering into a new life of relationship with the living Jesus Christ, we realize that we are entering into a newer, deeper, more intimate relationship with the living God—the God who is Father, Son, and Spirit.

Questions
- How do we relate to God as Father?
- How do we relate to God as Son?
- How do we relate to God as Holy Spirit?

God as Father

We relate to God as Father by being aware that God is constantly *present* to us, loving us, caring for us, providing for our needs, always merciful, understanding, and forgiving. Just as a very young child needs and wants the presence of his or her parents at all times, we rejoice in the continuous presence and availability of God as Parent—one who exhibits the qualities of both mother and father. This presence and availability is not the inhibiting and intimidating presence of a guard, not a "big brother is watching you" kind of presence, but a loving presence of one who gives us freedom and always seeks our good and our inner happiness.

God as Son

The tremendous idea that the Son of God is actually one of *us,* a member of our race, and part of the human family gives us a new perspective on our relationship with the Father, with Jesus, and with one another. Once we realize that Jesus, the Son of God, is truly human, we become aware that he is in very truth our brother—one who is eminently approachable. He is our elder, stronger brother who defends us, protects us, and intercedes for us with the Father. He unites us ever more closely with the Father and with one another as members of the same family.

Jesus made it very clear that he is identified with *all* humankind, that whatever we do or fail to do to another human being we do or fail to do to him. Therefore, as we relate to one another, we relate to the Son of God who is also the Son of Man. Regardless of race, creed, or physical or social condition we are all brothers and sisters of Jesus Christ.

God as Holy Spirit

Jesus promised to send the Spirit, who would be our advocate, our comforter, and our guide—the one who would remind us that Jesus is alive and active in our midst.

We relate to the Holy Spirit as the living, loving, and invigorating presence of the Father and Jesus in us and among us. The Spirit is within us as our *friend*. When we are most alone, alienated, lonely, fearful, prone to discouragement or despair, the Spirit is with us as consoler and strengthener. When we are in doubt or when faced with a difficult decision the Spirit, acting sometimes directly but more often through events and through other people, gives us the guidance, direction, and support we need. The Spirit is the Spirit of God's love, constantly warming, consoling, and supporting us—constantly helping us to think and act as Jesus thought and acted.

Questions
- **What difficulties am I apt to encounter as I strive to deepen my relationship with God—Father, Son, and Holy Spirit?**
- **How am I helped to enter into a deeper relationship with God—Father, Son, and Holy Spirit?**

Difficulties

Sometimes our scepticism makes it hard to accept the Good News. It simply seems too good to be true. A sense of our own unworthiness may tempt us to question whether even a God who is love itself can love me and forgive me and go on loving me in spite of my weakness and sinfulness. I may tend to demand signs, proofs, demonstrations from God, and, when these are not forthcoming, to lose heart and fall into disbelief.

It is easier to take refuge in legalism or to concern myself with *buying* God's love with attempts to merit that love through exact observance of laws, statutes, and prescriptions. It is more difficult to trust that God already loves me and to realize that I cannot (and certainly do not need to) *earn* God's love. The easier way is to attempt to gain assurance by my own efforts.

In the face of these tendencies, it helps to keep reminding myself that what God wants me to do is to *respond* to his love, to seek more and more to measure up to it. If I need further assurance that I cannot *earn* God's love (which is already there), all I need to do is read the Gospels and the epistles. Jesus was forever trying to make this point with the Pharisees. Saint Paul never tired of repeating it.

A rather serious difficulty may present itself, too—one which hits deep in my psyche. As I strive to deepen my relationship with God, I necessarily have to be honest with him. That means that I have to face up to myself and try to see myself as I really am. Such a confrontation can be very painful. It can be so frightening that I may simply refuse to consider it.

It will help to realize, in such a situation, that God already knows me as I really am and loves me nonetheless. A fearless self-inventory can have a liberating effect that will break the log-jam of my self-deception and put me on a plane of reality. This encounter with reality can give me the joy which comes from the realization that I am being really open and honest. It enables me to know and to accept that as I am *right now,* God loves and cares for me.

Special Helps

As I enter into this deeper relationship with God, I will discover many helps along the way.

1. *Greater hope and trust.* I will grow in my realization that God is my loving Father. He gives me the hope that I will never cease to exist. I will never be abandoned and left without help. And this realization is strengthened when I recall how often Jesus assures me that the Father loves me. He cares for and provides for all creation, but he cares so much more for me. This realization also prompts me to trust the Father as Jesus did. Jesus accepted death, trusting that he would rise to a new life. He assures me that if I trust God I, too, will rise and live forever.

2. *A better sense of my own worth.* A realization that God is my Father gives me a greater reason for self-esteem. While the expression, "Smile, God loves you," suffers from over-use, it is still very apt. The realization that Jesus is not a remote figure but my brother is a source of greater self-esteem. And the realization that the Holy Spirit is with me at all times can also give me a greater sense of security and worth.

3. *A desire to share the gifts I have with others.* When we are convinced of the reality of the love and activity of Father, Son, and Spirit in our lives, we feel a real urgency to reach out to others, to help them, and to show our hope. This urge to reach out and "spread the good news" is very evident in the Acts of the Apostles. As I read how the first Christians responded to the Good News, I feel impelled to do the same.

THE CHRISTIAN COMMUNITY

One of the greatest aids in answering the call to union with God is membership in the Christian community. The community in all its rituals and actions keeps alive the need for each of its members to grow in relationship to God—Father, Son, and Spirit.

The community addresses most of its formal prayers to God, the Father. In the context of those prayers, the community reminds its members of the creating and saving actions of God. The community strives to recognize and relate to Jesus in the sacraments—living signs of his action in the life of the community. We strive, too, for greater faithfulness to Jesus' command to love others as he has loved us. We recognize Jesus in the breaking of the bread. Members of the community receive the Holy Spirit in Baptism and are sealed in the same Holy Spirit in the sacrament of Confirmation.

The Christian community provides an environment which can be conducive to a personal relationship with God. Even the most simple and basic statement of faith, the Apostles' Creed, graphically reminds believers that we all relate to our God as a Father, as a Son and Brother, and as a life-giving Spirit.

PERSONAL PROFILE

Like any relationship, our relationship with God grows almost imperceptibly. To poke around at it too frequently can focus our attention more on the *fact* of the relationship than on the relationship itself. On the other hand, if we never review our relationship with God, we run the risk of taking it for granted. Use this opportunity both to express the relationship as you experience it, and also face in prayer the relationship as it is reflected in Scripture.

Review

Answer the following questions carefully. Express as best you can your feelings about and experiences of the action of God in your life.

1. Over the past six months, I have experienced my awareness of God as my Father in the following ways:

_____

_____

_____

_____

_____

2. Within the past six months, I have been conscious of Jesus as my brother and Savior in the following ways:

_____

_____

_____

_____

3. Within the past six months, I have been aware of my friend, the Holy Spirit, being with me and strengthening me in the following ways:

_____

_____

_____

_____

Prayer

God, my Father, always loves and cares for me. He is continually aware of me, my life, my pain, my joy. *Never* does he forget, ignore, or reject me. Select one of the following passages and probe its meaning for your life.

● *Psalm 139.* God, my Father, is always present to me and aware of me.

● *Isaiah 49:14–16.* God speaks: "I will never forget you. Upon the palms of my hands I have written your name."

● *Hosea 11:1–4.* He speaks again: "You are my child. I nurture you and teach you how to walk."

● *Zephaniah 3:14–20.* The Lord says: "I am with you. Rejoice! I will heal and restore you."

Jesus, our brother and Savior, shows his power and strength to us, his brothers and sisters. He calls us to be salt, light, and servants to others. Select one of the following Scripture passages and ponder its meaning for your life.

● *Matthew 5:13–16.* Be a force for good among the people with whom you live and work.

● *Matthew 5:38–48.* Love and serve others as I love and serve others.

● *Matthew 6:5–14.* Jesus shares with us and teaches us, his brothers and sisters, how to pray.

● *Matthew 18:15–18.* Resolve conflict with others with honesty and sincerity of heart.

The Holy Spirit, our consoler and our comforter, has been sent to us by Jesus Christ. He is our intimate friend. Select one of the following Scripture passages and ponder its meaning for your life and within your life.

● *John 14:15–18.* I will ask the Father to send you another Paraclete (teacher).

● *John 15:26–27.* The Spirit of truth. I will not leave you orphans.

● *John 16:4–16.* The Holy Spirit will prove the world wrong about sin, justice and condemnation.

● *Acts 8:14–25.* The gift of the Holy Spirit cannot be bought. Our relationship with the Holy Spirit is *gift*.

● *I Corinthians 3:16–17.* We are temples of the Holy Spirit. The Spirit of God dwells within us.

Preview

How do you *feel* about life after death? On the check list below, check off the words which express your thoughts and feelings. Add your own comments if you wish to do so.

Life after Death Is

____ spooky   ____ promised us

____ real   ____ foolish

____ scary   ____ reincarnation

____ a hoax   ____ sacred

____ a pious legend   ____ fullness of life

____ certain   ____ beautiful

____ great   ____ ugly

____ joyful   ____ decay

____ cruel   ____ a mystery

____ uncertain   ____ eternal

Now, in your own words, describe in some detail what you feel about Jesus' promise of a new life that will last forever.

_____

_____

_____

14 Jesus Calls Us to Eternal Life

A question we all ask many times during our lives and which becomes more important as we grow older is, "Is this life all there is?" Death raises the ultimate question about life. The potential I have to become a better human being is never fully realized no matter how many years I live.

What good, then, is it to strive to become a more humane person, to try to become as fully alive as I can if it all ends with the grave? I am important and unique. Does my uniqueness vanish from the universe the moment I breathe my last? Deep within myself I know that I am indestructible, but do I live on merely as a memory in someone else's mind? Science may reach deep into the mysteries of life and the universe and find the explanation of many of the things we now attribute to God, but science stops at death's door. At that point, faith offers the only satisfying answer to life's fundamental question.

Saint Paul found this answer in the hope for eternal life which Jesus offered to the world. He was eager to share the answer he had found with anyone who would listen. On one of his journeys he went to ancient Athens, which was the center of culture and intellectual activity at the time. The Acts of the Apostles says of the city and its inhabitants, "all Athenian citizens, as well as the foreigners who live there, love nothing more than to tell about or listen to something new" *(Acts 17:21)*.

Paul was delighted when the opportunity presented itself for him to speak publicly before an assembly in Athens. It was an impressive audience. Philosophers, teachers, students, men prominent in business and political life, educated people of various walks of life—all crowded into the Areopagus to hear this man who was creating such a stir among the people with his preaching about Jesus.

And the audience gave Paul full attention as he spoke of a God who was unknown to them. He was speaking in philosophical terms, in language they understood, and using thought patterns with which they were familiar.

But suddenly, as if an icy wind had blown through the vast stadium, the mood of the crowd changed. Some shook their heads in disbelief. Some laughed out loud. Others shouted in derision. The more polite simply smiled in pitying condescension. They expressed their feelings to Paul as they made their way out of the stadium: "We must hear you on this topic some other time." They offered a polite brush-off which is the equivalent of, "Don't call us. We'll call you."

Why this shocking, abrupt change of attitude? What was it that turned this interested audience into a derisive, mocking crowd? It was just a matter of a few words. Paul had been speaking about Jesus. All well and good so far. But then Paul stated that this Jesus of whom he was speaking had risen from the dead *(cf. Acts 17:22–32).*

To the people of Athens the idea of a resurrection from the dead was simply preposterous. Even among the Jews the idea was not universally accepted. It was, to be sure, a belief among the religious Jews. But one powerful Jewish sect, the Sadducees, rejected the idea completely. And even the apostles, who presumably did believe in a resurrection on the last day, were quite skeptical at first when confronted with the fact of the risen Christ on Easter Sunday *(cf. Luke 24:1–12, Mark 16:9–14, John 20:1–10, 24–29).*

Some of the early Christians, too, had problems about accepting the idea of the resurrection of Jesus and the resurrection of the just on the last day. The Christian community at Corinth, where Paul himself had established the

Church, provides a case in point. A dispute had arisen there concerning belief in the resurrection. Paul wrote to the Christians of Corinth:

> Tell me, if Christ is preached as raised from the dead, how is it that some of you say there is no resurrection of the dead? If there is no resurrection of the dead, Christ himself has not been raised. And if Christ has not been raised, our preaching is void of content and your faith is empty too. Indeed, we should then be exposed as false witnesses of God, for we have borne witness before him that he raised up Christ; but he certainly did not raise him up if the dead are not raised. Why? Because if the dead are not raised, then Christ was not raised; and if Christ was not raised, your faith is worthless. You are still in your sins, and those who have fallen asleep in Christ are the deadest of the dead. If our hopes in Christ are limited to this life only, we are the most pitiable of men.
>
> But as it is, Christ is now raised from the dead, the first fruits of those who have fallen asleep. Death came through a man; hence the resurrection of the dead comes through a man also. Just as in Adam all die, so in Christ all will come to life again, but each one in proper order: Christ the first fruits and then, at his coming, all those who belong to him.
>
> *(1 Corinthians 15:12–23)*

The point that Paul insists on is a vital one. Jesus spoke continually about life. "I came," he said, "that they might have life and have it to the full" *(John 10:10)*. And it is clear from his attitude towards life and from the way he spoke about it that Jesus saw life as one continuing, ongoing existence. He never spoke of physical death as the end of life but rather as a necessary step on the way to eternal life. And this eternal life he presented not as a pale, shadowy aftermath of our life on earth but as the full, whole, and complete existence that is our real and final goal. The problem is (and this is a problem that faced even Jesus) that there is no way we can describe this life, no way we can picture it. Saint Paul compares the fullness of life in the glorified state in heaven and the life we have in this world to an oak tree. Life here on earth, he tells us, is like an acorn. The life for which we are destined in the risen, glorified body is like the full grown oak. Realizing that all comparisons are pitifully inadequate, Paul had to content himself with paraphrasing the prophet Isaiah and saying, "Eye has not seen, ear has not heard, nor has it so much as dawned on man what God has prepared for those who love him" *(1 Corinthians 2:9)*.

Jesus, too, uses the analogy of a plant to describe the fullness of life for which we are destined after we have passed through death. "I solemnly assure you," he says, "unless the grain of wheat falls to the earth and dies, it remains just a grain of wheat. But if it dies, it produces much fruit" *(John 12:24)*. Then Jesus adds these important words, emphasizing that this fullness of life in heaven is not automatically acquired without any effort on our part. "The man who loves his life loses it, while the man who hates his life in this world preserves it to life eternal" *(John 12:25)*. This warning of Jesus is of tremendous importance. He, who loves, respects, and cherishes human life, is not saying that we should have no care for human life and the quality of life. Rather, he is saying that we must live a life of love, such as he lived and summons us to live, looking forward to our future happiness. We should not seek to make the present life our final and ultimate goal if we are to attain the everlasting life for which God has destined us. The only final death Jesus speaks of is that eternal state of death which is called damnation. Damnation would be the lot of one who chooses to separate himself or herself from God and his life-giving love. The fullness of life can be seen as the full bloom of a life lived in God's friendship—begun and nourished in its growth here on earth. Damnation can be seen as the final state of a life centered on self and impervious to God—begun and continued to the end of one's earthly existence.

Jesus said, "I am the way, and the truth, and the life" *(John 14:6)*. The summons he gives is the summons to learn of him, to follow his way, and to live as he lived. In this way we can pass through death to everlasting life. But Jesus does not merely talk about eternal life. He *shows* the way. He himself has gone through every step of the process that leads to the fullness of life. "If anyone would serve me," he said, "let him follow me; where I am, there will my servant be" *(John 12:26)*.

And the words Jesus spoke to his apostles at the Last Supper are the same words he speaks to all to whom he gives his summons today:

> Do not let your hearts be troubled. Have faith in God and faith in me. In my Father's house there are many dwelling places; otherwise, how could I have told you that I was going to prepare a place for you? I am indeed going to prepare a place for you, and then I shall come back to take you with me, that where I am you also may be. You know the way that leads where I go.
>
> *(John 14:1–4)*

Questions
- **How does the message of Jesus about the resurrection fulfill our basic human needs?**
- **What is the Christian attitude toward death?**

Our Basic Human Needs

The message of Jesus about the resurrection gives us the hope that our need for life, for love, and for meaning can be satisfied now, but will be *completely* satisfied only when we attain to the fullness of life after our death.

Our basic need for life can never be fully satisfied in this life. We reach the height of our powers and then decline. Yet our yearning for a full and satisfying life that will never end persists.

Our basic need to love and be loved can never be fully satisfied in this life, both because of our present limitations and those of others and because we and others must grow old and die.

Our basic need for meaning can never be fully satisfied in this life because of the limitations of our powers and because a lifetime is not long enough for the attainment of more than a relatively small degree of truth, knowledge, and wisdom.

The Christian Attitude

The Christian attitude is that death is the doorway to the fullness of life for which God has destined us. The Christian does not normally long for death; he or she values life as a great gift from God and seeks a full life for self and others. But the Christian sees death, when and in whatever manner God wills it to come, not as a tragedy—the end of hope, love, and life—but as a process which must be gone through in order to attain to a glorious resurrection and eternal life.

Questions
- **What difficulties do people have about belief in life after death?**
- **What experiences in our lives give us some indication of what death and resurrection may be like?**

Difficulties

When faced with the question of life after death, people encounter various difficulties.

1. Death appears to be the end of life. The decay and decomposition of the body seems to indicate the absolute end of the person. The complete silence from the other side of the grave, the total lack of communication with those who have died, seems to indicate that they have ceased to exist.

2. Material things, the things we can apprehend by our senses, seem to us to be the only real things. We cannot visualize a disembodied spirit or a glorified body, especially that of someone whose physical body has undergone death. gone death.

Moreover, the immediacy of this world makes it seem to us that this is all there is to life.

3. We have no certain way of imagining life after death. In the last analysis all we have to go by is our desire for immortality and a belief that relies on faith alone.

4. The things we have heard about heaven—symbols such as harps, wings, pearly gates, and streets of gold—may very well be found to be unappealing. Some people imagine heaven to be a never-ending prayer meeting or stuffy church service or an eternity of boring inactivity.

5. A confused idea about immortality is a problem for others. They think that they will come back to this earth in a reincarnation of some sort, or they think that they will live on merely in memory of the good works they have done. They cannot accept the fact that God loves them as unique, one of a kind, and that they will exist forever as the persons he created in personal fullness and wholeness.

The Experience of Leave-Taking

We all have experiences which give us an indication of what death and resurrection may be like. These experiences involve an ending, a leave-taking with its pain of loss that is followed by a pleasant and fulfilling new state or set of circumstances.

We have to move, to leave old friends and familiar surroundings, but find new friends and, perhaps, even new and better surroundings.

We grow up and, maybe with some regret, leave the things of childhood and youth behind, but find adult life more rewarding.

We are sometimes called upon to take a risk, to do something as yet untried by us, to "take a leap in the dark," relying only on the word of someone we trust, and find that we have grown and been enriched by what we have discovered.

THE CHRISTIAN COMMUNITY

When we attend a Catholic burial service, we may also experience something of the meaning of death and resurrection. Everything about the service speaks to us of hope, fulfillment, and the resurrection to a life of eternal happiness. The vestments are white—the liturgical color of joy. The prayers speak of life, peace, and eternal rest—contentment. The hymns recommended for the funeral mass are in the spirit of hope and consolation. The joyful cry of the *Alleluia* is heard throughout the service. Although the reality of the pain of loss and separation is by no means overlooked, it is met with a spirit of hope and a firm expectation of ultimate reunion and eternal happiness.

Sharing our hopes and aspirations with the people who share our faith helps us to grow in our hope for life everlasting. The whole Christian community, then, is a sign that Jesus will come again to call his followers to a new life with him.

PERSONAL PROFILE

Throughout this book, you have been recording your own reflections on your experiences and your feelings. It would be a good idea to go back and read everything you have written in this book. You should see a very comprehensive picture of where you are on the journey of faith. You can recall by this exercise how God has been calling you right now—at this moment of your life. This exercise can be a good reflection on what the process of **Becoming Catholic** is for you.

CONCLUSION

Welcome to High Adventure

These were the words which greeted you as you opened this book.

Now that you have finished the book, the question may well arise—how does "Becoming Catholic" involve such a thing?

Shouldn't it rather be—"Welcome to peace, to tranquillity, to a safe haven, to shelter from the turmoil and struggle of the outside world? Welcome to a Church that will give you all the answers, one that requires only a child-like acceptance of clearly defined doctrines, which answers all questions and demolishes all objections, to a Church that will enfold you in a nice, safe cocoon and give you the security that so many desperately seek in these troubled times?"

In the "Old Church," as the pre-Vatican II Church is often called, you might well have found such tranquillity, such a refuge from the world. But this was a Church still in reaction to the Protestant Reformation, a Church that was more a fortress, aloof and defensive, than a People living fully and realistically in a troubled, anguished but always fascinating world, a People very much aware of their involvement in a mission to that world.

Such is the Catholic Church today—alive, vigorous, often very exasperating, but vital, controversial, challenged, and challenging. It is no longer a Church of adults with the attitude of docile, unquestioning children. It is a Church which now accepts the fact that difference of opinion, the acceptance of responsibility, the right to speak up and express ideas, and, above all, diversity is the name of the game.

Adventure, in the last analysis, means the acceptance of challenge—the willing and zestful acceptance of challenge. This, of course, is the essence of the Christian message. And this, happily, is what the Catholic Church invites us to today. Those who are inclined to fundamentalism may yearn for a return to the security of a child-like state. But there is a dynamism inherent in the Christian message and in the Church. And despite tragic episodes in history and a necessary conservative element which always tends to temper new thought and new expressions of thought, the Church inevitably moves forward. The Church, despite such atrocities as the Inquisition, the Galileo case, and other indefensible historical events, does really stand today for freedom of conscience, the objective pursuit of biblical research, and that diversity which is still a basic characteristic of the Catholic experience. This is not to say that all Catholics want freedom of conscience, diversity of opinion, and full participation and involvement in the affairs of the world. But then, neither do all Americans want all the freedoms guaranteed by the Constitution and the Bill of Rights.

No matter. This is a part of the ferment that is going on within the Church today. And, unpleasant as it may be for some, it is a sign of vigorous life.

"Welcome to High Adventure," then, means "welcome to challenge, to struggle, to an ever growing realization of one's own woundedness and the sinful, wounded condition of the world we live in." But it means also "welcome to ever deepening growth as a person and as a Christian, to an active, sometimes exciting, often painful share in the mission to which we are summoned by the challenge of Jesus Christ." And it means, too, "welcome to a life of striving to attain that blessing of God's presence which Jesus promised when he said, 'My peace I give to you'—a deep-down peace which is, somehow, quite compatible with suffering and struggle—'that peace which the world cannot give.' " But such a blessing comes not with a superficial, "fellow-traveller" relationship with Catholic life. It comes only with real commitment and deep involvement.

The last verses of the last book of the Bible, the Book of Revelation, sum up very well the attitude of one who, hearing the call of God to a mission, realized that in spite of personal weakness and sinfulness, God's love is alive in that person's life. God's love leads us to find a new and more wonderful life in Jesus Christ. The writer of Revelation put the following words in the mouth of the risen Christ.

"Remember, I am coming soon! I bring with me the reward that will be given to each man as his conduct deserves. I am the Alpha and the Omega, the First and the Last, the Beginning and the End. Happy are they who wash their robes so as to have free access to the tree of life and enter the city through its gates.

"It is I, Jesus, who have sent my angel to give you this testimony about the churches. I am the Root and Offspring of David, the Morning Star shining bright."

The Spirit and the Bride say, "Come!" Let him who hears answer, "Come!" Let him who is thirsty come forward; let all who desire it accept the gift of life-giving water.

The One who gives this testimony says, "Yes, I am coming soon!" Amen! Come, Lord Jesus!

The grace of the Lord Jesus be with you all. Amen!

(Revelation 22:12–21)

Design and Production
T.R. & Associates-Tom Carbonel
Phoenix, Arizona